The Simple Guide to Buying Your New Home

How to Buy the Right Home at the Right Price in Any Market

Written By

Kwe Parker

Chapter Contributions By

Mimoza Cejku, Audrey Veitch, William Wormley, III

LEGAL NOTICES

The information presented herein represents the view of the author as of the date of publication. Because the rate with which conditions change, the authors reserve the right to alter and update their opinion based on new conditions. This book is for informational purposes only. While every attempt has been made to verify the accuracy of information provided in this book, neither the authors nor their affiliates/partners assume any responsibility for errors, inaccuracies or omissions. Any slights of any person or organizations are unintentional. If advice concerning legal, financial or any other real estate related matters are needed, the services of a fully qualified professional should be sought. This book is not intended for use as a source of legal or accounting advice. You should be aware of any laws, which govern business transactions and/ or other business practices in your country and state. References to any person or business, whether living or dead, are purely coincidental.

STATEMENT OF EARNINGS/DISCLAIMER- Every effort has been made to accurately represent this product and its potential. Examples in these materials are not to be interpreted as a promise or guarantee of earnings. Earning potential is entirely dependent on the person using our product, ideas and techniques. We do not purport this as a "get rich scheme."

Your level of success in attaining the results claimed in our materials depends on the time you devote to the program, ideas and techniques mentioned, your finances, knowledge, and various skills. Since these factors differ according to individuals, we cannot guarantee your success or income level. Nor are we responsible for any of your actions.

Any and all forward looking statements here or on any of our sales material are intended to express our opinion of potential. Many factors will be important in determining your actual results and no guarantees are made that you will achieve results similar to ours or anybody else's. The guarantee is based on the actual purchase price of the book, proof of payment and documents to show that the program was followed.

ALL RIGHTS RESERVED- No part of this course may be reproduced or transmitted in any form whatsoever, electronic, or mechanical, including photocopying, recording, or by any informational storage or retrieval without the expressed written consent of the authors.

Printed in the United States of America

Meet Kwe Parker

A skilled mortgage professional is both knowledgeable and adept in identifying clients' needs. Growing up in a working-class Baltimore community taught Kwe Parker the importance of hard work, integrity and helped formulate the compassion he uses to guide people through financial transactions. This may explain why Kwe views his mortgage banking career as an opportunity to help people fulfil their dreams of homeownership and show them ways to leverage real estate to build wealth.

Kwe Parker has over 18 years of real estate finance experience and he is a graduate of Marylhurst University, one of the nation's only real estate finance curriculums. Whether home improvement lending, FHA rate reductions or luxury home construction mortgages, Kwe has a rare diversity of experiences to help clients with simple and complicated mortgage needs. Since 2003, he has originated and managed over $1 billion dollars in mortgage originations nationwide.

He released this book to answer the many questions that potential home buyers frequently have when contemplating buying a home.

Professional Memberships & Affiliations

1. National Association of Mortgage Professionals
2. National Association of Real Estate Brokers - *Affiliate*
3. National Association of REALTORS - *Affiliate*

Kwe Parker – *Real Estate Expert, Author & Speaker*
NMLS #49165
Website: www.KweParker.com
Social Media: @kweparker
Media Information & Booking: media@kweparker.com

TABLE OF CONTENTS

PREFACE

Many consider homeownership the American dream. In fact, property ownership is a well-known builder of wealth in our culture. For those contemplating homeownership today, the risks of declining values, fears of buying a maintenance headache, and the countless problems associated with the mortgage crisis have made the dream far less enticing.

Many of you know or have heard of people that have either had difficulty purchasing a home or lost homes due to foreclosure. I commend you for setting aside the negative possibilities in light of the most probable gains. Despite the recent housing challenges, homeownership still offers tax benefits, protection against rent increases, and the ability to invest your money in a fixed asset. Owning a house gives one the ability to truly create a home.

Without a doubt, purchasing a home may be the biggest financial commitment some people will ever make. Sadly, most first-time buyers do not know where to start when beginning the process. This leads them to blindly trusting real estate agents, banks, and other professionals, instead of familiarizing themselves with the process. I believe that people should not only have the right to homeownership, but also have the right to get accurate information from credible sources. An informed consumer ultimately makes the best homeowner.

After handling thousands of mortgage transactions I have experienced the pleasure of being able to help people become homeowners. I have also advised countless people through their fears, doubt, and inaccurate information that they received from friends, family and unreliable Internet sources. My goal was to give them the best information to enable them to make the best-informed choices.

By no means will reading this book protect you from every possible buying trap. Nevertheless, it will give you a firm foundation to build upon and help make a potentially complicated experience rather simple. Unlike most home buying books, this book is not an elongated sales letter nor does it provide complicated in-depth analyses of real estate transactions. There is not an abundance of jargon and complicated terminology. The sole purpose of this book is to help homeowners make the best choices.

This book is created with the first-time buyer in mind. I apologize for the over emphasis on simplicity. When writing this book, I felt that this book was not the forum to showcase my perspectives on the latest economic trends that impact the mortgage and real estate markets. This book was not the platform to impress my peers with unique perspectives on the housing crisis.

Instead, my goal was to provide relevant instructions to new home buyers, with the hopes that the horror stories do not deter potential buyers from pursuing their dreams. I also want to ensure that buyers are not vulnerable to the predators that lurk. Although I appreciate the college professors and consumers that have published instructions to consumers on home buying, I believe that experience has value. Few authors of similar books are actively working in the industry, have the hands-on experience and possess the real estate-related education to provide up to date information that new buyers can use.

I want you to enjoy this book, but more importantly I want you to heed the advice provided. I would love to credit my own intellect with this information. To do so would be dishonest. There were countless contributors that referred clients, helped me perfect processes, and worked beside me over the years. My team also contributed greatly to every chapter. These people are the true authors.

As I transition into this book I encourage you to follow the guidance provided in these chapters, but I also challenge you to follow your heart. A house may be a financial investment, but a home is a family and emotional cornerstone. You will not be able to quantify every benefit of owning a home. You will need to listen to your heart and instincts. Then rationalize it with your calculator. A home that is good from an investment perspective, but bad for your lifestyle is ultimately a bad investment.

In this one-of-a-kind resource you will learn the importance of:

1. Asking questions and uncovering a treasure chest of information about your prospective home, the seller and your real estate team.
2. Making a decision based on the "90/10 Rule." Ninety percent will be the facts that you are presented with and ten percent will be listening to your gut feeling and following your heart.
3. Being confident in yourself, because you have the knowledge, tools and resources to walk with your head high and make your own decisions.

By investing in this book you opened the door to an entire library of information about buying your home. The provided information will serve as guiding lights on your journey. Throughout the course of this book you will notice many references to online resources that accompany this book. The checklists, letters and, tips will accelerate you on your path to becoming a home buying expert.

CHAPTER 1

Introduction
How the Most Popular Home Buying Practices
Often Lead to Very Costly Mistakes

John and Mary are a couple from Maryland. They came to meet with me about buying their first home. During our meeting, they explained that this was not their first attempt to purchase a home. Four years prior, they attempted to buy a home, but ended up with no house, a lot of wasted time, thousands of dollars spent and they were days away from being on the street with their two children. Needless to say, after they shared their story, it was apparent that it took a lot of courage for them to even meet with me to revisit the possibility of buying their first home. I commended them for taking that step.

Their previous transaction began when Mary contacted her sister to suggest a good real estate agent. The agent that her sister recommended was her sister's longtime coworker at the post office, who had sold real estate part-time for over 10 years. They called the agent, went to meet her at her office, and immediately started home shopping the next day.

They looked at numerous homes of all sizes, types, and price ranges. After a few months of searching, they found the ideal property. It was in a nice area. The school district was perfect for their kids, so this seemed like the perfect first home.

Under their real estate agent's guidance, they pre-qualified for a mortgage with a local well-known bank. Then, they placed a contract on the house. The sellers accepted the contract, so

John and Mary put the wheels in motion and moved forward to giving the real estate agent $1500 as a down payment, paying for the appraisal, purchasing their homeowners' insurance and paying for a structural and mechanical inspection of the house. The lender even provided them with a closing date.

After a few weeks passed, the day of settlement was approaching. Between packing up their apartment and shopping for items for the new house, John and Mary were excited. Then, they received the phone call that shattered their world. It was their real estate agent. The real estate agent explained that their loan was declined.

Their immediate reaction was disbelief. John and Mary were patrons of that bank for several years. Their credit had always been strong. Besides, the bank stated that they had been preapproved and John has a letter as proof.

"There must be an error... there is no way that this can be true... I'm going to get this straightened out right now," John shouted. John hung up the phone, grabbed his jacket, his meticulous loan folder and his keys. Tears started to run down Mary's face. "Mary, I am going to that bank to clear things up," he said while scurrying to gather items he may need to resolve the issue. Then, he headed out the door.

While driving to the bank, he calls his loan officer, Dan, from his cell phone. John and Dan had developed a good rapport throughout the process. In the back of his mind he knew Dan would straighten things out. One problem, he can't get Dan on the phone. All he gets are voicemails.

John pulls up to the bank. When he explains the situation to the branch manager, the branch manager informs him that Dan, his loan officer, was on vacation for 2 weeks. John asks the branch manager to help.

"Why am I being told that my loan is being denied?" asked John. The branch manager offered to check;

leaves the room for a few minutes and then returns. Here is when things get interesting.

The branch manager returns and confirms that the bad news was accurate. He then goes on to explain how John's overtime hours were not consistent enough to be considered for loan qualifications. As a result, John and Mary did not have enough income to get the loan. He apologized and encouraged them to reapply in six months.

"How is this just becoming an issue and I submitted my documentation 3 weeks ago?" asked John angrily. The bank manager sympathized with the scenario, but went on to explain their review process. Although Dan, his loan officer, reviewed the file, he was not an underwriter. Apparently, Dan assumed that John's overtime hours could be used, issued the pre-approval letter, and then was later informed of his error.

The branch manager walks John out and he calls his wife and real estate agent to inform them that they were indeed denied for the loan. "I know a lender that can get this done... give me a shot at fixing this," their real estate agent said in an attempt to prevent John and Mary from losing all hope. Minutes later she had John and Mary back on the phone with a new mortgage lender.

The new lender sounded optimistic. Since their real estate agent had worked with him in the past, this seemed hopeful. John made sure to explain his overtime situation and emailed some documentation to the loan officer, while they were on the phone.

Things seemed solid. After about 40 minutes on the phone with the new lender, the loan officer provided great news. They were approved. John, Mary and their agent breathed sighs of relief. "Are you sure?" the real estate agent asked the loan officer. "Everything is solid... all I need is proof that they have the 10% down payment to close and we can close in as little as 3 weeks," said the loan officer.

The real estate agent then explained confidently that she had located a grant for John and Mary, so the down payment was not a factor. According to the housing counselor, all they needed to put down was $1000. The loan officer went on to explain that this was not the case. This new lender did not participate in the down payment assistance program that John and Mary were relying upon to buy a home. In addition, the lender went on to explain that what they all believed was 'free money' was essentially a second mortgage. Not only would that bank not accept that grant program, but the so-called grant money that was available, was repayable with interest in the future.

The real estate agent connected them with more lenders, in an attempt to get the deal done. However, the efforts were not successful. Despite paying for an appraisal, an inspection, and then terminating their lease, they had no house and no contingency plan for an apartment. Their landlord had already found a new tenant. Their all-American homeownership dream had turned into a nightmare.

By John's recollection, they spent over $2500, between the appraisal, insurance, inspection, and the moving company deposit. Most of these fees were non-refundable. Having no money or time to risk pursuing the purchase further, the couple decided to cut their losses, gave up trying to buy a home, and proceeded to locate an apartment.

Although their story was an emotional rollercoaster, it was not shocking. After 20 plus years in real estate finance, I have heard countless horror stories. As Mary and John, alternated telling parts of the story, I could almost anticipate what they would say next.

Fortunately, I was able to help John and Mary purchase their first home. They closed in less than 2 weeks and everyone else told them the soonest they could close was 30 days. In addition, they used my home buyer strategy and saved $2400 off of their lowest loan offer. Despite their nightmare, there was a happy ending for them. Nevertheless, the happy ending does not negate the fact that many of the problems they experienced in their first attempt at home ownership could have been avoided, with the proper guidance.

I have shared this story many of times to hundreds of clients. Why? The realities of the possible hazards are not necessarily apparent to people when they start the home buying process. The Internet is filled with shady sales people masking half-truth sales pitches as unbiased information. Some real estate agents will tell you anything to get their next commission check. And unfortunately, many lenders will lie, cheat, and give you a last-minute heart attack at the closing table when you see that the bottom line doesn't remotely resemble what you were initially told.

Homeownership is by far one of the greatest wealth building tools and an accomplishment that I wish for every family. However, there are vultures dressed as trusted advisers that will gladly help separate you from your hard earned money. This is why it is necessary to educate yourself on the process and possibilities.

I wrote this book for two reasons...

> 1# - My clients had many questions and I wanted to recommend a book that was easy to read, up to date and provided information that really worked. The last thing I wanted to suggest was some book written by a finance professor that had never done a transaction.

> #2 – A book of this sort did not exist!

I have always believed that educated home buyers make the best homeowners. This is why I provide tools and resources that give the consumers simplified information. As a result, the consumer is more confident, comfortable and ultimately has a basis to appreciate the level of service that we provide. So...

How is John & Mary's story relevant to your home buying experience?

If you cannot identify things that are wrong, how can you identify what is right? If you cannot identify problems in a mock scenario, there is a strong probability that you will be susceptible to the same pitfalls. This is where education becomes essential.

At the end of this book, you will be able to identify not only the mistakes that occurred in John and Mary's first transaction, but you will also be able to identify how to make your home buying process smooth and headache free.

There are two lines of thought when buying a home, the popular path and the efficient path. Like most things in life, the majority is often wrong. Things change daily, markets shift, and loan programs are discontinued. You need to know enough to make the best choices.

What This Book Will Do For You

Simply put, this book will give you solutions to your most troubling real estate questions. But more importantly, within the pages of this book I will reveal simple-to-follow home buying strategies that allow people to benefit from years of insider real estate secrets, tips and strategies. What you hold in your hand are the exact answers to questions you may have, but most likely do not even realize you will need answered, until you are well into your home buying process.

Remember that the information within these pages are taken straight from my "Preferred Home Buying" seminars that I offer to my first-time home buyer clients. I have used and continue to use this system to advise my clients on how to get the most for their money with the least headaches. You now have access to the same information that has worked for thousands of clients. I hope that you will utilize this information to the maximum and later share with me how it helped you through your home buying experience.

CHAPTER 2

There is Never a Bad Time to Buy
How to Buy a Home With Confidence, Like the Pros, in Buyers' & Sellers' Markets

After years of helping hundreds of buyers discover the joy of homeownership, I can say I have pretty much heard people speculate on reasons why the market conditions made it less than ideal times to buy real estate. Many question, "Am I too young?" or "What if I lose my job?" Then there are affordability questions, such as "Why can't I find anything in the price range that we are pre-qualified to buy."

My many years of helping home buyers find answers to those questions means that I am uniquely qualified to give you a simple yet effective way to blast right past those excuses. After reading this book you will know with 100% confidence that right now is probably the best time for you to buy a home. Now, let me give you some information about the unique benefits of buying a home in this economy.

Why Buying Your Home In Today's Economy Still Makes Good Sense

Here is a little pop quiz to get us started. Do you know how many homeowners lost their home in foreclosure because of the reported 300+ or more mortgage lenders going out of business from 2006 to 2011? Well, if you watched the news and listened to the media you would think the answer is hundreds of thousands or possibly millions of homeowners lost their homes due to lenders going belly-up. However, the real answer is none, zero, and zilch.

"Not one homeowner lost their home due to the mortgage industry collapse."

Most people incorrectly assume that the mortgage debacle caused homeowners to go into foreclosure and lose their homes, but it is actually the other way around. Homeowners, who for any number of reasons, were unable to make their monthly mortgage payment greatly contributed to the mortgage collapse. The reason why homeowners did not go into foreclosure because of the mortgage industry collapse is because their mortgages were insured. Every person who lost their home to foreclosure during the mortgage collapse was simply unable to make their monthly payment because of rising mortgage payments, loss of job, or some other misfortune. The fact of the matter is, if those homeowners had the money to make the payment they would still be in their home today.

It is this unfortunate abundance of folks who recently lost their homes that now provides a tremendous opportunity for you today. There hasn't been a golden opportunity like this for a long time. You could probably spend another twenty or thirty years waiting for the same window of profit potential that we have now.

When you get down to the nuts and bolts of how you can invest in foreclosures during these economic times, it comes down to these facts; you must buy homes at a bargain price that you can continue to afford even in a worst-case scenario. You must use a fixed interest rate mortgage that never increases, while squirreling away enough emergency money for a rainy day fund.

Regardless of all the pressure to keep paying rent until the market gets better, there is still no debate that buying a home today provides great tax advantages. It is also still true that owning your own home allows you to build wealth and provides security and stability for your family. Those benefits do not change regardless of what the market is doing. They are truly timeless.

The Benefits Package Homeowners Enjoy

When you feel those brand new house keys in your hand and hear that little soft jingle in your pocket after buying your home, you will feel like a brand new person with a renewed passion for life. There are few joys in life that come as close and there are some very good reasons why you should feel so good. Buying a home gives you access to wealth by building equity when you or your tenants make your mortgage payments, while having something tangible that you own to show for it and is the gateway to a multitude of tax breaks.

Example: Jane stumbled across a good deal when she bought her first home. Her manager told her about a home on his street that he'd watched slip into foreclosure over the past several months and eventually was listed on the market for sale. She ended up buying her house for $185,000 when it was actually appraised for $215,000. She pays $1250 per month towards principal.

> Principal Amount = $185,000
> Market Value = $215,000
> Equity = $30,000 ($215,000 - $185,000)

The Best Thing Since Sliced Bread...Almost

As you make your monthly payment and begin living your new life, you slowly begin to accrue something called home equity – simply by making your payment. Equity is the difference between what you owe on your home and the market value. Building equity means that as you pay your mortgage, the principal amount (the total amount you borrowed) of the loan decreases and the home value could go up. Many people have been able to retire and live a comfortable life as millionaires because their home built up so much equity over the course of their lives. As a result they then sold their home, took the money and launched their own successful business. However, before you begin seeing dollar signs, I must also warn you that sometimes the home values decrease for any number of reasons.

Goodbye Landlord...Hello Home!

I am convinced there is no better feeling in the world than telling your landlord that you are moving into your new house next month so he or she will not be able to fund their retirement plan with your hard-earned dollars.

This feeling alone is truly priceless.

Seeing Where Your Money Is Going

One of the many joys of homeownership is that each and every month you actually get to touch, feel, see and smell your money. This means that you can actually track where your money is going and it forces you to save money each month by paying your mortgage payment and building equity.

This is a forced savings plan, which provides a roof over your head.

It's All Yours!

The first several months of waking up in your new home will flood your mind with a flurry of emotions. The thought most often shared by new homeowners is the overwhelming feeling of, "Is this is all mine?"

You Finally Catch A Tax Break

Everyone dreads paying taxes, but when you are renting, you have a higher level of dread when April 15th rolls around. Well, when you own a home you might actually begin to look forward to tax time because you begin to hear that old familiar cash register cha-ching sound.

Here is why: You get to deduct your mortgage interest as well as many other items such as:

Points
Home Equity Loan Interest
Property Taxes
Interest on Home Improvement Loans
Home Office Expenses
Prepayment Penalties
Upfront MIP (if applicable)
Moving Costs

Having these additional deductions means thousands of dollars in tax savings for you each and every year. Pretty sweet, huh?

As if that was not enough, when you sell your home after living in it for two of the last five years, you do not have to pay taxes on the first $250,000 of profit that you make when you sell your home. But wait it gets better. For those of us who have joined our lives together in holy matrimony we get to keep $500,000 tax-free.

Thanks Uncle Sam!

The Top 10 Excuses You May Be Tempted To Use To Procrastinate From Buying Your Home...

Now, since I call planet Earth my home, I know sometimes in life we all get a little discouraged or overwhelmed with large financial decisions. So, in an attempt to help you out, I will provide answers to some of the major excuses you might begin to tell yourself to stop from buying a home and the few times you might absolutely be right in doing so.

Excuse #1: "I am Afraid To Buy Because The Economy Is Bad."

While it is true that the economy is not bustling with activity, thousands of people just like you are preparing to make their best move. After all, these are the very same circumstances that cause "buyers markets." A buyers-market simply means that there are more houses for sale on the market than there are available buyers who can purchase them. As a result home sellers are more willing to be flexible with price, terms and extras in order to get their homes sold.

Your number one goal in a bad economy is to buy smart, insure yourself, your home and your income, and make sure you have substantial savings in the bank before AND after you purchase your home. Buying your home this way will help ease any fear you have of the market doing a nosedive once you move into your new home.

Excuse # 2: "I do not know what to buy...I'm confused."

This is a common concern for many prospective home buyers, so let me give you several ways to get clarity quickly. The first tip is to follow your gut and listen to your instincts. If you are constantly drawn to condos because of little to no maintenance then think of the reasons why you feel this way and go with it. You *should* be looking for condo. Do not try to convince yourself to buy a raised ranch with a huge backyard, which requires ongoing maintenance.

The next tip is to keep an open mind while visiting a variety of properties. This will allow you to narrow down what you do not like and will give you the confidence to recognize what you do like instead of second guessing yourself. I don't mean to get philosophical on you, but follow these two steps and you will begin to see a clear path where there was only confusion before.

Excuse # 3: "I Don't Have Enough Money For The Down Payment."

When I hear this excuse I automatically know it usually means the house the buyer really wants, requires more of a down payment than they currently have. It is also important to keep an open mind and seriously consider downsizing to the amount of down payment you can afford.

Excuse #4: "But I Don't Know Anything About Home Maintenance Or Home Repairs."

Well, join the club. There are millions of folks who flock to Home Depots across the nation each weekend to take classes on plumbing, painting and gardening. Additionally, some of the most popular television shows are based on fixing up, repairing and improving your home. Get ready to become an expert user of your DVR for more than recording reruns of old Friends episodes. Buying a home is more like a journey than a destination. You will have plenty of time and practice to become the handyman or handywoman you've always wanted to be.

Excuse #5: "...But, What If I Lose My Job?"

Unless you are planning on buying your house cash, then you must join the millions of hardworking Americans who manage to keep a job and pay their bills. If you are that concerned about losing your job, then I would strongly advise you to find a career and job in which you can feel more secure.

We both know that you will always have to maintain some form of income to support yourself and your family, regardless if you buy a home or not. So, why not have something to show for all those years of working very hard? Additionally, you should really take some time to learn about disability, unemployment and mortgage insurance coverage in case of financial disasters.

Excuse #6: "I Actually Enjoy Renting..."

Now, you might be one of the few people walking around who actually enjoys making your landlord wealthy while you sweat and toil for every penny. If that is you, put the book down and slowly back away before I jump through the pages and put you in a headlock until you yell "Uncle!"

However, if you are like the rest of us, then you enjoy the

luxury of keeping more money in your own pocket and the freedom of not stressing about where you live. Those luxuries and freedoms are virtually nonexistent when you are renting. By renting you will always be paying someone else for the right to have the illusion of living a life of luxury and freedom, but at the end of the day you know deep down in your heart your landlord is the one really calling the shots.

Excuse #7: "I Can't Afford A Home..."

When you say you cannot afford a home, what you really should be saying is that "I cannot afford a home that costs $400,000, but I *can* afford a home that costs $225,000." You can use this fill in the blank formula whenever this mood overcomes you. It quickly snaps you back into the reality that it is about the size of the mortgage you can afford.

When it comes to affording a home you should always remember it is as easy as adjusting the mortgage amount and maybe taking a little longer to save for a down payment.

Excuse #8: "I'll Wait Until I Am Married..."

There is no good reason why you should wait for Mr. or Mrs. Right to come along before you begin getting all the great benefits of homeownership. Get started today! My advice is that you should be looking for a smaller home and consequently a smaller mortgage if you are going at it alone.

Yes, I know there is a chance of meeting Mr. or Mrs. Perfect five minutes before your closing, but if he or she really is "the one" for you then he or she will recognize your potential by watching you handle the responsibility of homeownership.

Trust me when I tell you that owning a home is a feather in your cap to a prospective spouse.

Excuse #9: "It is Way Too Much Responsibility..."

Can you remember when you first learned to drive?

Remember worrying about cars in front of you…cars in back of you…keeping your hands on the wheel…and watching the rear view mirrors?

The first time you do anything you will be threatened with fears of feeling overwhelmed, but do not give in to those fears. The financial obligations of making your monthly payment are the same as when you are renting. You pay or you do not get to stay regardless if you are renting or owning. The difference is in the painting, mowing and managing the repair guys when you need work done.

Don't sweat it. It's not rocket science. You can do it.

Excuse #10: "This Pep Talk Is Great…But I Am Still Scared"

Let me be the first to tell you this in case you have not heard it before. It is very likely **YOU WILL BE SCARED THE ENTIRE TIME!** There…it is out of the way. I am not going to try and do a Jedi-mind trick on you and tell you that you should not be afraid. It would not matter anyway because you would still be scared. The fact of the matter is EVERYONE is shaking in their boots when buying their first home, but you can minimize the fear when you have the knowledge, tools, resources and a great real estate team supporting you.

That is what this book is all about: Giving you the knowledge, tools, resources and showing you how to pick a world-class team of real estate experts to guide you through the best and biggest financial decision of your life.

On The Other Hand, Renting May Be Your Best Option If…

- **Renting may be your best option if…your income will be dramatically less soon.** However you may still be able to afford a smaller home or condo, but you should wait until your new level of income is determined.

- **Renting may be your best option if…you need to have options.** If you spend half the year in Italy and the other half in Spain then you only need a hotel room when you are in town to repack for the next move. You most likely do not need a 2,500 square foot raised ranch.

- **Renting may be your best option if…you are moving cross-country within months.** If your ideal dream of living the good life is hauling your entire life back and forth cross country several times a year, then owning a home may hold you back from your dream life.

- **Renting may be your best option if…owning a home costs you three times what rents costs in your area.** There are some parts of the country where you really have to be a millionaire to buy a home. In this case you have two choices: continue to make the rich even richer by paying rent or buy in a different town or neighborhood.

- **Renting may be your best option if…you honestly do not have two nickels to rub together.** There are always costs to be paid out of pocket for the appraisal, home inspection, etc. For example, when you moved into your apartment you needed a security deposit. Well, buying a house is an even bigger decision than renting an apartment so you also need to have *at least* two to three months of mortgage payments.

Smart Home Buyer Program
Step #2

1. Write down the top three benefits you will get from buying your home.

   Benefit # 1 _____

   Benefit # 2 _____

   Benefit # 3 _____

What is Coming Up Next ...

In the next chapter you will learn how to have laser-point precision when matching your needs and wants to your ideal house. This will save you tons of stress and hours of wasted looking at homes that do not work for your goals so continue to read...

CHAPTER 3

Your Reasonable Wish List
Identify & Communicate What Your Family Needs and Wants in a House Before Shopping

Regardless of the real estate market, in most towns and cities there are more than enough housing options to suit every home buyer. For example, for the last few years if you were looking for a townhouse or condo, you could pretty much find the pick of the litter for less than what you would pay in rent for an average two-bedroom apartment in most areas. By the same token, if you were searching for a nice single family home instead of a townhouse or a condominium, and perhaps you are in a position to start a family, you would do well to consider where you could find a home for an average sales price of under $350,000. However, the real issue facing most first-time home buyers is how to find the perfect home for their needs, wants, and future plans with a price tag they can afford.

The first step in finding your dream home does not start with spending all of your free time driving back and forth from open houses. The first step you need to take in order to find your dream house is to focus on yourself. When I say yourself, this also includes your significant other, children, extended family (pets) and any other important influences, which will be impacted by the decision. This process starts at your current residence, while sitting down watching television or over dinner. In this chapter I will cover a multitude of variables that you may or may not have considered during the home buying process. I am sure there will be some that may apply to you that I have not listed. Therefore, use what I provide as an outline and a guideline in regards to determining your needs. However, you will need to follow this process to come to a decision without jeopardizing your down payment money needs.

One of the major challenges facing most home buyers is future planning. Usually, as a renter you are only required to look twelve months into your housing future because you were most likely just signing a twelve-month lease on an apartment. However, when you are in the process of purchasing a home, the time line of what you must consider is longer as well as it should be. You must think about the new place of residence in a longer term; we normally suggest seven to a ten-year period. In addition to the time consideration, there are also additional factors such as your lifestyle, family plans for the future, convenience to job and your neighborhood to name a few.

The Wonderful Rediscovery of Yourself And Your Family

The first step on the path of finding your dream home is knowing exactly what you personally want and aspire to do with your new home. It is vital that you hone in on exactly what your lifestyle needs and wants are. For example:

- **Are you planning on living alone, with spouse, or small family?** Consider the fact that life sometimes sends us unintended expansion projects (i.e: pregnancy) to test our flexibility. An extra bedroom would be really valuable.

- **What are your plans for the home?** Know your goals. You may want to run your own home-based business, so you may need an extra bedroom/home office or a nice little garden or patio that you've always dreamed about.

- **What lifestyle choices do you need to adhere to?** By the time you are old enough to buy a home there are some amenities you just do not want to give up. Take this into consideration when looking at homes. As a first time home buyer, it is important to figure out the definite wants versus needs. Make a list of must haves and things that you may be okay not having.

- **What is a day or night like at home for you?** Are you the kind of person who would rather curl up and read a book all day in a quiet place in your home or do you prefer the loud thumping bass of techno music? Are you handy with home repairs or do you just run for the phone book as fast as you can anytime there is a problem?

House Features

When it comes to the tangible elements of your ideal home you will want to start with some of the good and bad elements of the apartment or house you are living in currently. Maybe you love the hardwood floors in the living room and kitchen, but cannot stand walking on cold floors in your bedroom. Or perhaps you have discovered that you have a better outlook on life when your bedroom window faces the sunrise. The list can go on and on, but I am certain that you have already discovered some of your ideal amenities throughout your years of renting. That is a good source to draw from to put together a list of must-have features in your prospective home.

Here is a list to get you started:

General
House Style
Square footage
Number of bedrooms
Number of closets
Number of bathrooms
Car Garage
Ideal Home Age
Types of flooring
Fireplace
Central Heat/Air

Updated house systems (plumbing, electrical or mechanical)

Floor Plan
Number of floors (two story etc.)
Great room
Formal living room/dining room
Basement/Attic
Laundry room
Family/Den
Home office

Kitchen
Spacious or compact
Type of flooring
Eat-in
Automatic Dishwasher

Outside
Large yard/big lot
Fenced in property
Pool/Spa

Neighborhood Niceties

When considering a neighborhood you must view it in terms of neighborhood niceties and your neighborhood exit strategy. These are the intangibles and tangibles that make a community nice to live in. Such as:

- **Safety and Security** - Knowing that both you and your biggest investment are safe at all times.

- **Welcoming Community** – You would not want to move into a community that views new residents as parasites sucking the blood from their veins. You want to feel that you are a part of something good.

- **Convenience Factor** – How close are you to work, schools, shopping centers, grocery stores etc. There is nothing worse than your gas tank being on "E" and there is not a gas station for twenty miles in either direction from your house.

- **Education Factor** – If you already have kids then you know how important being in a good school system is to your child.

- **This Neighborhood Does Some Weird Stuff Sometimes Factor** – There are some neighborhoods that require you to paint your house certain colors and restricts you from painting it any other color or pay a fine. Imagine that.

Neighborhood Exit Strategy

When selecting a neighborhood you always want to think about resale value. By keeping resale value in mind when purchasing your home, you will not be forced to spend months and months on the market if and when you decide to sell your home.

A fast and easy way to determine resale value is to judge how well the house you are buying matches the neighborhood you are moving into. For example: You do not want to own the only townhouse in a multi-family neighborhood. Chances are the majority of buyers who would be purchasing your home are looking for multi-family investment properties. The single-family home buyer would feel like they are still renting and probably does not want to live in another transient renter's neighborhood.

Another method of putting together an exit strategy is to think about the very things you are looking for as a home buyer. Young couples have been buying homes since the beginning of time and not much has changed. The usual suspects are good schools, clean streets, close to necessary places of business, etc.

Brand New Home Vs. Not-So-Brand New Home

Every home buyer I have ever met had an image in their mind of what they want their home to be like. Some people want the traditional green lawn with the white picket fence, while others dread any type of manual labor and elect to go with a professionally maintained condo community. At the end of the day, the only thing that matters is that you choose a house you could live with…figuratively and literally.

There are basically two groups of houses you will be considering:

Brand New Houses/New Construction

The best part about buying a newly constructed house is that you are the first to leave your mark and make it a home. Other benefits are:

- **Environmentally Friendly** – Most of the new homes are built to save energy and with sustainable materials.
- **Updated Everything** – If you are a gadget loving person you will have to restrain yourself from going overboard with customizing your new home. Many add on expenses beyond what they initially budgeted.
- **Custom Made Just For You** – The best part is that YOU designed it and seeing your vision come to life.

The down side of new construction is:

- **Cost an arm and a leg** – Thanks to inflation and cost of goods rising, it usually costs more to build a home, than it does to buy that same home if it was already built. This is a really important factor to take into consideration of your home buying process.
- **Pushy salespeople** – These are the folks hired by the builders to move these houses so they are very aggressive and eager to sell you.
- **You are breaking everything in** – Nothing has been tested for longer than thirty seconds to make sure it is plugged in and there are bound to be some kinks in the system to be worked out. Usually, brand new constructions will have a warranty with the home, but you have to decide on whether or not you want to be the first to work out the kinks.
- **Patience is a virtue** – Builders rarely finish homes on time, so be prepared to dig in for the long haul. This is not to bring down the construction industry; it is to simply understand that there are factors in the equation that no one can control.

Not-So-Brand Spanking New Houses

Older homes tend to have some unique benefits that many home buyers really enjoy like:

- **Better prices** – Older homes usually have lower sales prices.
- **Personality** – Homes seem to develop character over time as they age.
- **Stable Neighborhood** – The community is built and functioning before you move in. Remember the resale value we mentioned earlier.
- **Tested Construction** - The majority of homes have their issues in the first couple of years so you get to skip that fun part.

The down side of buying an older home is:

- **They usually sell for less later on** – Most home buyers want newer construction when possible
- **Less efficient** – Older buildings do not preserve energy as well as the new material construction does.
- **Smaller rooms/closets** – Older homes were built in a different time, before the new standards that everyone wants. For example, walk-in closets in every room as opposed to just the master.
- **Costs of repairs** – Appliances and materials tend to need to be repaired/replaced right after you move in because time has done its number on the house.

One Big Happy Family...Or Not

Everyone is familiar with the single-family house and condo. However there are three types of housing structures that are broken down into communities. This means when you buy into a community there are certain responsibilities the community at-large provides for you and then there are certain responsibilities you perform for the community...mostly in the way of paying their monthly fees.

The three major type of housing communities are: condominium associations, planned development associations (PUD) & town homes and co-op associations. I will break down the benefits of each so you get a good understanding of each if you are considering going this route.

Condominiums

When you buy a condo you own the inside of your home, but not the common areas such as swimming pools, stairwells, gardens or sidewalks. Those areas belong to everybody. Owning a condo makes sense because:

- **Less work for you as a condo owner** - the condo association takes care of regular upkeep and maintenance so you do not have to. No snow shoveling or grass mowing.

- **Being part of a community** – this can be a blessing or a curse depending on your neighbors but, all in all it should work out okay.

The ugly side of living in a condo is:
- The over-abundance of rules, regulations and fees
- You paid less so, you also make less when you sell
- Big brother or neighbor is always watching and listening
- You must pay those fees each and every month or get fined
- The inability of the condo owner to control the increase in condo fees

Planned Development Association (PUD)
When buying a PUD, they are generally single-family homes. Sometimes they developments are gated or just have a sectioned off entrance to the development. Common areas are sometimes common in PUD developments as well. Such as: play grounds, pools, streetlights, benches, or pet walking areas. Whether or not there is a homeowners association, depends on when the community was constructed. This does not mean that a community could not agree to create an association if there is not one in existence. If there is an association fee it is generally less than an association fee for a condo since it covers less accommodations and services. Homeowners are generally responsible for their own yard maintenance and snow removal.

Town homes (Or Townhouses)
When you buy a townhouse you are actually buying more than a condo so you should expect to pay more than for a condo. Here is why: With a townhouse you actually get title of ownership to building and the land upon which it sits.

Sometimes the only visual difference between a condo and the townhouse is that the townhouse is usually vertical with two floors, but that is not always true. Whether or not there is a town house or a home owners association, depends on when the community was constructed. This does not mean that a community could not agree to create an association if there is not one in existence.

Co-Ops: The Good, The Bad And The Ugly
When buying a co-op you are really buying shares of a corporation that in turn owns the building you are living in. This really means that you are renting from the corporation and as a result are bound by rules that at times seem only one step removed from renting. As a result of buying shares of the corporation you are required to vote in order to make any real changes. And of course you must pay a monthly membership/maintenance fee. As a first-time home buyer you should probably steer clear of co-ops.

Smart Home Buyer Program
Step #3

1. Sit down with your spouse, significant other, or by yourself and map out exactly what you are looking for in a home.

2. Ask your friends what they think you would like in a home. Expect to be pleasantly surprised.

What is Coming Up Next ...

In the next chapter I reveal how you can uncover exactly how much house you can afford before talking to a loan officer or any real estate agent while calculating your monthly mortgage payment so continue to read for more...

CHAPTER 4

Getting the Most for Your Money
Determining How Much House You Can Afford vs. How Much House You are Qualified to Purchase

Figuring out how much you can afford can be really simple. However, if you do not have the right instructions to follow then figuring out how much you can afford can be as complicated as debating who has the best tasting slice of pizza. In this chapter I'm going to review how you can calculate how much you can realistically afford, but more importantly I will show you how to calculate how much a mortgage lender will approve you for in a three-step system consisting of:

1. Calculating how much you can comfortably afford each month including ALL of your monthly debt payments.
2. Calculating your maximum monthly mortgage payment from a lender's perspective.
3. Coming up with a maximum purchase amount.

Knowing Your Cash Flow And Total Expenses Before Buying A Home

The first step in knowing how much you can afford is to know your current money flow for your household. So that requires you to take a snapshot using the good old handy-dandy expense budget. Now before you do this necessary step, I want you to know that you may very well be surprised by how much you are currently spending each month on nonessentials, but then again that is why you are doing this now and not later.

There are two ways to use this housing budget and both ways are valid methods of figuring out your monthly cash flow. The first method is to examine your previous full month of income and expenses and use those to fill out the budget. This method is simple, if you do most of your banking online, pay your bills with your debit card or pay bills electronically from your account.

The second method is to start from today and track your spending for a full thirty-day cycle. This method is most useful when you operate your household on a cash payment basis or you do not have a clue what each specific payment is on your bank statement. Meaning, you pay primarily everything with cash.

Housing Cash Flow Sheet	
Item	**Monthly Income**
Income (after taxes are taken out)	
Salary/wages/tips (you)	
Salary/wages/tips (spouse)	
Alimony	
Child support	
Pension or other retirement	
Rental income (net)	
Interest or dividends	
Other income _____	
Other income _____	
Total Income:	
Expenses	**Monthly Payments**
Charity	
Clothing	
Credit card payments	
Education	

Entertainment	
Food (groceries and meals out)	
Gifts	
Automobile payment(s)	
Utilities (electric, gas, etc.)	
Home telephone, cable, cellular	
Insurance – auto	
Insurance – disability (if not with employer)	
Insurance – life (if not with employer)	
Insurance – long-term care (if not with employer)	
Insurance – other	
Prescription medicine	
Contribution to savings – "rainy day fund"	
Misc. money spent	
Subscriptions/dues	
Transportation – gas, oil	
Transportation – maintenance	
Transportation – public, tolls, etc.	
Miscellaneous household expenses	
Other expenses _____	
Total Monthly Expenses (without rent payment)	
Total Monthly Income	
Total Income minus Total Expenses	

Once you finish your Housing Cash Flow Sheet, then you will know your maximum amount for your monthly mortgage payment. The number that you are left with at the bottom of your Housing Cash Flow Sheet is the MAXIMUM monthly payment you can afford each month. Completing this worksheet allows you to know the true amount you can afford each month regardless of how much a lender will approve you for a purchase price.

This step is very important because at the end of the day YOU are the one paying the mortgage payment. YOU are the one working the extra hours to pay bills. So YOU should be the only one to determine what YOU truly can afford. There is no reason why you should become the next Channel 8 News special because you became one of the thousands of homeowners who fell into foreclosure six months after buying a new home.

> **EXAMPLE:** Russell and Liz have a combined total after-tax income of $4,400 per month and total expenses of $2,600. That leaves them with $1,800 per month after expenses and savings. Therefore they can afford to comfortably spend $1,800 on their total housing payment. That payment includes (P)rincipal, (I)nterest, (T)ax and (I)nsurance, also known as PITI. They were able to purchase a condo for $200,000 with five percent down and payments came in under $1,800 per month.

From A Lenders Perspective: How Much You Can Afford

In Mortgageville, PITI stands for principal, interest, taxes and insurance and is pronounced the same as pity. Here is what it technically means:

> **(P)rincipal** – The amount you borrow and still owe after making monthly payments.
>
> **(I)nterest** – The percentage you are paying the lender on the money you borrowed.
>
> **(T)axes** – The property taxes on the house you buy as determined by the city, town or village.
>
> **(I)nsurances** – The hazard (and possible mortgage) insurance you pay each month.

When you add them all up you come up with the acronym called PITI. There are two very strong words of caution for first time home buyers when it to understanding how PITI affects you. The first is the PITI is always more than what you expect it to be when estimating your numbers alone at home in front of the computer. The only time these numbers are really clear are after you find a home and sign a purchase and sales contract.

The second word of caution is for co-op or condo buyers. If that describes you, then you will have to add in additional association fees and possibly an additional insurance payment to the equation as well.

When you are doing your calculation at home you cannot possibly have an idea of what taxes and insurance might be, but do not feel too bad because as soon as you find a home you will be able to calculate the final numbers. Mortgage lenders are also in the same boat as you when they are first approving you for a maximum purchase amount. They simply estimate what you will need based on their previous experiences.

Comparing Your Housing Cash Flow To A Lenders Ratios

Over the years there have been many times when I have seen mortgage lenders approve buyers for larger mortgages than they can actually afford. And no I'm not talking about the "liar loans" which allowed loan officers to lie about a buyer's income. I'm talking about legitimate applications when mortgage lenders review your previous years W2s, current paystubs, and current credit report and STILL overestimate how much you can afford. This happens because a mortgage lender does not know your actual household expenses like you do. That is why it is important to complete your Household Cash Flow Sheet BEFORE you get preapproved or prequalified for a mortgage. You will know pretty much down to the dollar how much you can actually afford each month regardless of a mortgage lender's approval.

As you are reviewing the lenders ratios be sure to keep in mind that at the end of the day you will be the one making the mortgage payment. Therefore, you will need to be the final authority on how much of a mortgage you will personally sign off on.

Additional Costs To Consider When Calculating What You Can Afford

When purchasing a home it is important to remember to count the total cost of homeownership. Otherwise, you will find yourself with plenty of house, but little to no money to purchase necessities like furniture, appliances or even maintaining your home. By knowing and planning for the true cost of homeownership you can sidestep some of the usual landmines most folks face. There are three basic groups of additional costs you should be prepared for and they are:

- The down payment
- Out of pocket upfront costs to close on the home
- Regular expenses to stay in your home

Down Payment

As of the time of this writing the average home buyer is required to put down at least three to ten percent. However, if you are coming up a little short in this department then you will be happy to know there are some great down payment assistance programs for home buyers which can cover all or a portion of your down payment and closing costs.

As recently as three years ago, many home buyers balked at the advice that they should save up and put down ten, fifteen, or twenty percent like back in the good old days. However, in the wake of the mortgage and banking industry collapse there has been a revival of the age-old tradition of putting down a large deposit. As with many old folk tales there is a softball size grain of truth in the wisdom. There have always been benefits to putting down a sizeable down payment when buying. When you contribute a down payment of twenty percent or more towards your home purchase you get certain benefits such as:

- Lower mortgage payments, because you borrowed less money for the mortgage.

- Lower interest rate, because of less risk to lenders because you have skin in the game.

- Paying less interest, because you borrowed less money.

- No Private Mortgage Insurance (PMI) – PMI is for mortgages generally over eighty percent of the value of the home at the time of purchase.

So you may want to think twice about trying to finance as much of your purchase price as possible because you can get a better deal when you use more of your own money.

However there are some times when using up your cash for a down payment is not the best choice, no matter how good the mortgage rate will be. I'm talking about the times when leaving a huge down payment will leave you with little to no emergency funds, force you to walk to work and eat peanut butter and jelly sandwiches for a year. There are also other cases in which it does not make sense to put up to twenty percent down. A twenty percent down payment can be a prince's ransom when you are buying in certain areas where the homes can easily cost up to $750,000. A twenty percent down payment in those cases would mean almost two hundred thousand dollars, which is a big check to write any day of the week.

Out of Pocket Costs

The next arena of costs related to buying a home range from a couple hundred dollars to the thousands. The good news is that most of these costs can be financed within the loan itself, but there are others you will have to pay upfront and they are:

- **Appraisal & Home Inspection Fees** – The appraiser and home inspector have to be paid at the time their services are issued and these costs could add up to be over one thousand dollars.

- **Closing Costs Including Points** – This is the biggest cost factor in the entire process because this could easily run eight to ten thousand dollars. On the other hand, these are usually financed within the loan so don't get stressed out. However, there are times when you may have to bring money to closing to pay these costs.

- **Moving Costs** – Unfortunately no one is going to box up your apartment, rent that U-Haul and gas it up for you. This one is on you.

- **Utility and Service Costs** – You might be able to simple get your service transferred to the new place, but invariably there are always some companies who require deposits.

- **Repair or Improvement Costs** – Unless you buy a brand new construction home, you will have to fix or change some things as soon as you move in. You need to have an emergency or reserve fund for when this happens.

Ongoing Costs

When it comes to ongoing costs of owning a home it is important to keep in mind that much like your car a home also needs many forms of regular maintenance. Just to give you an idea of what to expect The major ones are roof inspections every several years, updated electrical or mechanical systems, and landscaping to name a few. Some of the other ongoing costs include:

- Yard maintenance
- Updating housing systems as needed (electrical, mechanical, plumbing)
- Replacing indoor fixtures and appliances
- Improvements or overall changes to your home
- Real estate taxes
- Homeowners insurance

Smart Home Buyer Program
Step #4

1. Complete your Housing Cash Flow Sheet and calculate your Debt-To-Income ratio

What is Coming Up Next ...

In the next chapter, I reveal how you can learn your credit scores and making sure your credit scores are high enough so you are able to be approved for the lowest fixed interest rate on your mortgage so continue to read for more...

CHAPTER 5

Painting the Best Financial Picture
Understand Your Credit Profile and Learn Shortcuts to Improve Your Credit and Financial Picture…Position Yourself to Get the Best Loan Possible!

Your credit scores are one of the most important factors that lenders use to determine your ability to qualify for a mortgage and your down payment needed.

In fact, in this challenging economy you probably won't qualify for a mortgage program in the first place unless your credit scores and history are up to par. It is an unfortunate reality that many people do not truly understand what their credit scores reflect and how their credit scores can affect their ability to gain access to the best loan programs available.

In this chapter, I will break down the fastest and easiest way for you to manage your credit. I will explain exactly what you need to know about your credit scores in order to purchase your first home using the minimal down payment required. After reading this chapter you will have the exact step-by-step blueprint to increase your credit scores at will or just better understand your current credit situation.

Credit Score Basics

Your personal credit scores are three digit numbers ranging from a poor score of 400 to an excellent score of 850. Your credit scores are the result of many factors that ultimately "tell a story" about how well you pay back money you have borrowed.

Mortgage lenders use these three credit scores to determine your willingness and ability to repay your debts.

Mortgage lenders gather your credit scores from three major credit bureaus that monitor over 40 different components to come up with a number for your credit scores. However a company called Fair, Isaac and Company (FICO®) acts as a mediator between the three major credit bureaus and your mortgage lenders which is why you will see the credit scores referred to as FICO® scores. It is important to know that the three credit bureaus are separate from FICO®, whose job is to make sure the scores from all three credit bureaus use a standard procedure to be calculated. The three major credit bureaus are:

- Equifax FICO – BEACON score®
- Transunion FICO – EMPIRICA®
- Experian FICO – Experian/Fair Isaac Risk Model®

Mortgage lenders rely on these companies to determine what type of mortgage they can offer you because it gives them a pretty accurate picture of your trustworthiness. For example, if you have a credit score of 720+, you can get a mortgage with an interest rate that is below the average rate for a normal home buyer without paying any extra fees for that rate. One such example of fees you may be able to avoid when your scores are above average is loan discount points.

Paying a point means that if you are borrowing $200,000 then one point would be $2,000 (200,000 x .01) Therefore, loan discount points are dollars that are added to your financed amount or paid out of pocket to get the interest rate of your mortgage reduced.

Having a high credit score also means you will most likely qualify for par rate, which is simply the lowest interest rate you qualify for without paying money to get it lower or any behind the scenes money being paid to the mortgage professional.

Credit Score Guide

Here is a credit score guide to give you an idea of what to expect from a lender depending on your credit scores:

720-higher   A   You get the best interest rates for conventional, conforming and FHA or VA home financing, and expect to pay minimum costs for your mortgage.

620-719   B   You qualify for conventional, conforming and FHA or VA financing, but you are viewed as a slight credit risk. You should expect to pay a higher interest rate and slightly higher fees when getting a mortgage.

580-619   C   You are right on the bubble and getting a mortgage approval will require a manual review by an underwriter. You may not qualify for conventional or conforming, but FHA and VA may still be an option for you. You should expect to pay higher interest rates and higher loan fees.

400-579   F   If you are here then it is time to go back to the drawing board and regroup. You definitely need to get some help with increasing your scores before proceeding with purchasing a home. However, a lender may be able to help set you on the right path.

How Credit Reporting Bureaus Calculate Your Credit Scores

The three major credit bureaus Experian, Equifax, and Transunion look at all of the credit that you as an individual have listed on your credit reports. Their window of time goes back for the last ten to twelve years in some cases. This includes loans, credit cards, bills, bankruptcies, foreclosures and judgments, tax liens and credit inquiries or requests that have been made in the last six months. What they are looking for is how you have made your payments – on time, always late, delinquent, etc. They will also look to see if you have enough of a credit record to even generate a score. The three bureaus use different methods of calculating this number, which is why your credit can be perfect with two of the bureaus and not so perfect with the third.

Here are the important factors that the credit bureaus take into consideration when calculating your credit score:

35% - payment history
30% - amounts owed
15% - length of credit history
10% - new credit
10% - type of credit use

Based on those percentages you can see how it is important to have the specific information on how you score in each area prior to purchasing your home. However, there are three common myths that I want to dispel about how credit bureaus calculate your scores:

1. Mortgage lenders do not average all of your scores together and they use the middle score to qualify you for a mortgage and down payment program.
2. Married couples do not share the same credit scores. Each individual is treated differently based on his or her own contributing factors.
3. Each credit bureau will have a different credit score because they each put a different importance on individual factors.

Credit vs. No Credit

Over the years I have heard many people say to me, "I just pay everything with cash and so I do not need credit." I wish that were true, but unless you have millions and millions of dollars in cash it is not. I always make sure that I tell them that your credit scores reflect how well you pay back money you have borrowed, but if you do not borrow any money, companies do not have any way of knowing how well you pay your debts back. So it is very important that you monitor, nurture and grow your credit scores very much like a gardener will nurture a bed of roses.

Your credit score allows mortgage companies and other loan companies to determine whether or not you are a risk or a good investment. They analyze your credit history to see if you meet the minimum acceptable guidelines the lender has in place that they grant loans by. If your score meets the requirements, an underwriter whose job it is to manually look over your mortgage application and all of the documentation you provide to the lender, will review it and determine what kind of interest rate you now qualify for.

If You Do Nothing, Here is How Long Your Bad Credit Hangs Around	
General Credit Information	Seven years
Collection	Seven years from date of last activity
Bankruptcy	Seven to ten years
Foreclosure	Up to twelve years from the date filed
Garnishment	Twelve years from the date or entry or seven years from the date satisfied
Judgment	Twelve years from the date or entry or seven years from the date satisfied
Tax Lien	Twelve years from the date or entry or seven years from the date satisfied

Dismissed garnishments, judgments, and tax liens	Not reportable.

***There are no legal requirements for credit bureaus to keep this information for so many years, but they do it because they want to!**

Here is an overview of who uses your credit scores:

- 99 of the largest banks in the United States
- 49 of 50 largest U.S. credit card issuers
- More than 400 insurance companies
- More than 150 retailers
- 9 of the top 10 retail card issuers in the United States
- More than 80 government or public agencies
- More than 100 telecommunication carriers
- 49 of the top 50 global banks

Information obtained from www.fairisaac.com/fairisaac/company/clients

Who Sold My Credit?

We like to believe that our credit information is at least safe at the credit bureaus. However over last several years a dirty little secret has come out. The credit bureaus sell your private information to whoever is willing to pay a few bucks. They claim that they only sell your information to give advertisers and businesses a better understanding of ideal candidates for their products.

What is The Minimum Credit Score To Buy a Home?

The mortgage professionals who assist you with your mortgage will submit your application and credit reports through an automated underwriting system called DU. This computerized system will instantaneously review all of your pertinent information and notify the mortgage professional within seconds with a decision. The computerized system will give you one of two possible outcomes, which are: Approved or Refer (Denied unless manually underwritten.)

If your mortgage professional notifies you that your application was "referred" don't be too discouraged, because mortgage lenders can sometimes make exceptions when you have compensating factors. For example, if you have fifty or seventy-five thousand dollars in your savings account when you only need fifteen thousand for the transaction; that is viewed as a compensating factor. It is also viewed positively if you have been at your current employer for a long period of time, i.e. 20+ years. There are several other compensating factors so speak with your mortgage professional before giving up hop

"But I don't owe anyone a dime..."

It was not Nicole's fault. No one had taken the time to tell her that no credit is oftentimes just as bad as having bad credit. So she was really devastated to learn that she did not have any credit scores. That meant she did not get an automatic approval for a mortgage.

Jason on the other hand was prepared for bad news. He'd spent freshmen year of college learning the meaning of "plastic money." Surprisingly it was his early experiences that made him resilient. He was positive, smiling and optimistic about taking the action steps needed to improve both their scores.

It took them about 90 days and a couple of hours of putting together information showing that they'd paid their bills on time for the last three years. The results were amazing. They were approved for a low fixed rate mortgage as a result of their hard work. Good job folks!

How To Overcome Credit Challenges As Quickly As Possible

Unfortunately finding mistakes on your credit report is a very common problem. Many people are not aware they have a problem until they are denied over and over again after having what they *thought* was good credit. Here is a sobering statistic: Close to half of the population in America has erroneous information on their credit reports. Because computers are used to aid underwriters in determining whether or not a loan should be issued, many people are undeservedly denied credit.

This is one of the reasons why some mortgage lenders will allow customers to review their credit report and submit letters of explanation as to why things are on there. When this happens, customers stand at better chance of getting approved. Additionally, some mortgage companies or loan brokers for mortgage companies will help you fix the problems on your credit report, especially if you pre-qualify for a loan and have the time to work on it while looking for a house.

WARNING!

Do not purchase your credit scores directly from Experian, Equifax or Transunion. It may shock you to know that the scores they give you are not the same credit scores which lenders use to approve you for a mortgage. You should only get your credit scores from FICO® directly because these are the only scores which matter!

Some of the most common errors and mistakes include:
- Credit cards and debts that do not belong to you on your report.
- Late payments that were never actually late.
- Loans that you never took out.
- Former spouses that are still carrying the other's line of credit on their reports.
- Credit lines that were never used, but are still showing as being open, such as department store credit cards.
- Bankruptcies, foreclosures, tax liens and other judgments that have been completed, satisfied or

discharged but never changed to reflect the status on the report.

- Old loans that were co-signed where the guarantee is no longer needed.
- Previous use of a consumer credit counseling service that has been completed that is not reflected properly on the report.
- Identity theft

Information obtained from www.fairisaac.com

Who Sold My Credit?

We like to believe that our credit information is at least safe at the credit bureaus. However on the last several years a dirty little secret has come out. The credit bureaus sell your private information to whoever is willing to pay a few bucks. They claim that they only sell your information to give advertisers and business a better understanding of ideal candidates for their products.

6 Steps To Increase Your Credit Scores And Create The Life You Have Always Wanted

Having low credit scores in today's economy is like trying to swim in a pool with bricks in your pocket. You may be able to swim for a short time but after a while your legs get tired of kicking and you have to get rid of the bricks. You may be able to get along for a while with bad credit, but at some point you are going to need a new car, an appliance or as we are discussing now; a new home. The six-step system I'm giving you allows you to improve and increase your credit scores in the least amount of time possible with the help of trained experts. Yes, you can do it yourself, but by the time you learn all of the ins and outs of credit repair you could have had the higher scores already. After many years of helping dozens of normal hard-working folks fix their credit here is my recommendation:

1. **Purchase your official FICO® credit scores**

   You will have to pay a small one-time fee to use this service but it is worth every penny. You get immediate results to the exact information mortgage lenders will be using to approve you for a mortgage as well as the 12 reasons why your credit scores are so low. It is one thing to get low scores, but it is more valuable to know the reason for the low scores.

   You can go to www.annualcreditreport.com and receive your credit reports for free if you do not mind waiting 45 - 60 days. The only downside is that you do not receive the 12 reasons your scores are low and by the time you receive the reports so much has already changed on your credit reports.

2. **Hire a credit expert repair company to help repair your credit**

   This is the most basic step that I recommend to anyone who has a low credit score and several negative accounts that should be removed.

3. **Follow each and every step of your customized credit repair plan prepared by your own personal credit repair expert.**

   When you make the decision to bring in the credit experts you are committing to the first step in improving your credit scores. However, the most important step is when you actually do the plan that the experts create for your unique situation. It would be wrong of me to tell you that you only have to make one phone call and it is taken care of for you. The reality is you will have to continue to pay your bills, abstain from making new unnecessary ones and manage your finances better.

4. **Purchase your FICO scores every 90 days to make sure your old scores are being updated with improved scores.**

   I cannot overstate the importance of continuing to

purchase your updated credit scores every 90 days. It is vital that you track and monitor your progress all the way to the finish line. Purchase your credit reports every 90 days to continue getting your official FICO® scores which won't cause your credit scores to go down because of the inquiry.

5. **Sign-up with a credit monitoring service that advises you instantly by email and text message any time there is a change on your credit reports.**

   Subscribing to a credit monitoring service allows you to rest easy knowing that you will be made aware of any negative or positive activity on your credit reports. The best part about credit monitoring is that you won't be penalized for inquiring into your own credit reports.

6. **Be patient and do not get discouraged, because it may take several months to see a drastic improvement!**

   If it took you four months to increase your credit scores to 675, 683 and 701 would the four months be worth the wait? Some people feel that five years of bad spending habits should only take thirty days to fix, however you must be realistic. It will all be worth it when you can go to any car dealer in the area and qualify for a zero percent interest loan for the car you have always wanted because you have great credit. So do not give up on your dream!

Credit Repair For The Do-It-Yourselfers

If you are determined to repair your credit without the help of experts, here are some steps to follow. First, request your credit reports from each of the three major credit bureaus. After you receive your credit reports the next step is to decide which items you want to dispute. You will start by listing the errors, omissions or problems and then write dispute letters for the incorrect items to each credit bureau where the item appears incorrectly.

Be sure that when you mail in the dispute letter you should include who the credit account was with, the account number listed on their report and why you are disputing it. In your letter ask the credit bureau to investigate the claim and then remove the information from your report.

By law, the credit bureaus must remove derogatory information that they cannot confirm with the listed vendor within 30 days of receiving your letter. Make sure to ask for an updated copy of your report at the end of your letter to ensure that the credit bureau complied with your request. Review your credit report annually to make sure it remains up to date and correct.

Bonus: Quick Tips To Increase Your Credit Scores Immediately!

Here are some of the surest ways to increase your credit scores before, during and after buying a home:

- Know all three of your scores
- Avoid unnecessary inquiries
- Only use lenders that report your credit limit accurately
- Pay off your credit cards each month
- Do not max out credit cards each month
- Verify that lenders report correct payment history each month
- Stay away from finance companies
- Keep credit accounts open
- Do not believe that income can overcome every credit problem
- Bank/Debit cards won't help your credit rating
- Do not co-sign for another person
- Use credit instead of cash
- Pay down debt instead of shifting it
- Maintain a few major credit cards

- Increase your credit limits regularly
- Eliminate mistakes on your credit reports
- Apply for credit at the right time
- Avoid debt consolidation loans
- Ignore preapproved offers in the mail
- Use the credit you have
- Pay your bills early or on time.
- Keep a mixture of credit accounts

Smart Home Buyer Program
Step #5

1. Purchase your official FICO® credit scores.

2. Print out and keep your three credit scores where you can always access them. This allows you to estimate your interest rate before meeting with the mortgage lender.

What is Coming Up Next ...

Now that you are armed with your budget and credit scores you are ready to go get prequalified for your mortgage. The next chapter tells you exactly how to qualify for a mortgage without losing the shirt off your back while getting the lowest possible interest rate so continue to read for more...

CHAPTER 6

Mortgages 101 – More Than Just Rates
Demystifying Mortgages to Help You
Understand How Rates, Points & Fees Impact
Your Bottom Line

This chapter is designed to be a detailed look at the entire mortgage process and serve as a step-by-step plan to help you get the best and lowest interest rate possible.   There is immense value within the next several pages so be sure to get a pen, paper or write within the pages as certain things are sure to stick out. Just by reading these pages you will be more than prepared to attend your meeting with your mortgage professional with confidence. It is also the time when you reap the rewards from all the hours of reading books, saving money and hours of hard work.

So with that in mind we will go back to school.   Except this time it is Mortgage University.

Everything You Ever Wanted To Know About Mortgages…And Then Some

Let's start with the basics: A mortgage is when a bank loans you money to buy a house. The word mortgage is also interchangeable with the phrase home loan. Now as you can imagine, no one except maybe your immediate family is in the business of loaning (or sometimes giving) money away without expecting a return on their investment.   Therefore banks charge interest on their loans as well as numerous fees and points. A point is one percentage point of the total loan amount. ($200,000 x .01 = $2,000)

The Two Types of Mortgages

No matter how creative Wall Street bankers get, the fact of the matter is there are only two types of mortgages; fixed or adjustable. You can further break those two down into various types of fixed and adjustable, but the essence always remains the same.

There are two little differences that can further separate fixed and adjustable. The first difference between fixed and adjustable is called conventional or conforming mortgages. The second difference is called government insured mortgages.

Conventional means the borrower and the mortgage amount falls within a specific set of guidelines and requires that the borrower put down a substantial down payment. The guidelines for conventional or conforming mortgages tend to be strict and unforgiving when it comes to lower credit scores or a small amount of savings available to use for your down payment and closing costs.

Government insured loans means that the U.S. Housing and Urban Development Program (HUD) offers a federal insurance program, which provides extra protection against default for the mortgage lenders. These programs include Federal Housing Authority (FHA), Veterans Administration (VA) and U.S. Department of Agriculture Rural Development (USDA) loans.

It is much simpler to think of all mortgages as fixed or adjustable, so that you can keep the insanity out of your mind. I have given you the major terms, phrases and definitions that you need to know to make an informed decision. If you are like me, then you don't want to worry about the dozens of variations of these two types of mortgages.

So, here is a simple guide to help you:

1. **Fixed Mortgages** – Includes 30, 25, 20, or 15 year term periods. With fixed mortgages, you always make the same payment each month. You just choose how long you want to be paying the same payment. There are also fixed balloon mortgages which are fixed for a period of time but then require you to make a lump sum payment all at one time at the end of the loan term. Balloon mortgages are pretty scary…even from a mortgage professional's point of view.

2. **Adjustable Rate Mortgages (ARM)** – These mortgages do just what their name implies – adjust. You may have one month, one year or ten years, but at some point they will adjust. What the mortgage lenders do to come up with an adjustable mortgage rate is borrow money from huge global banks such as the London Interbank Offer Rater (LIBOR), the 11th Federal Home Loan Bank District Costs of Funds (COFI), U.S. Treasury Bills, or Certificates of Deposit (CDs). Whatever the interest rate those global banks charge the mortgage lenders is referred to as the *index*. The mortgage lenders then add on their profit markup to the index and the profit markup percentage that is called the margin.

   Here are some of the more popular ARM programs:

- ***Traditional ARMs*** – The interest rate starts out with a low rate to entice you to sign-up (called a teaser rate), then begins its slow or not-so-slow climb upward each month or whatever agreed upon time frame you selected.

- ***Interest Only ARMs*** – You only pay the interest each month for the specified time period you selected and when the time lapses you begin paying the additional principal and interest payment.

- ***Option ARMs*** – You get four options each month of what you want to pay.

  1. Minimum monthly payment
  2. Interest-only payment
  3. 30 Year payment
  4. 15 Year payment

  It seems like a good option at first, but the biggest risk is that most people end up paying the minimum or interest only payment and end up owing more than the property is worth. This happens because the lenders just add what you are supposed to be paying to your loan balance. They then adjust your payments every year to reflect the new loan balance. This is called negative amortization. It is really just playing a game of Russian roulette in Mortgageville.

- ***Hybrid ARMs*** – these are usually shown as 3/1, 5/1. 7/1 or 10/1. This means they are fixed for 3, 5, 7 or 10 years and then adjust every year after the specified period of time.

  If you thinking of choosing an adjustable rate mortgage then you need to know the following before you sign:

- *Starting interest rate:* This is your initial interest rate.

- *Adjustment period*: Your option of having your rate change monthly, biannual or annual. If you choose this mortgage you should always choose annual.

- *Index*: The cost for your mortgage lender to borrow the money. You should choose a slow changing index life (COFI) because as your lenders index rate goes up so does yours.

- *Life-of-the-loan cap*: This is highest interest rate your mortgage will go up to.

- *Periodic cap*: This limits how much the interest can adjust in a one-year period.

- *Low margin*: This is the mortgage lenders profit margin should be around 2.75 percentage points.

- *Prepayment Penalty*: A penalty for paying your mortgage off early. Usually around six month's worth of mortgage payments. There should never be a prepay penalty – why should you get penalized for paying off your mortgage sooner?

- *Negative amortization*: When you make the minimum monthly payment it is actually lower than what you really owe. The difference between the minimum payment and what a regular payment should be is added to your total mortgage at the end of the year. You could end up owing more than you borrowed when you make the minimum monthly payment.

- Assumability: You may be able to sign over your mortgage to your home buyer when you sale – it is called an assumable mortgage when this happens.

Interest Rates

When buying a home the interest rate is one of the most important factors, so I will give you some insider tips and suggestions. So, here are three pieces of information you should know about the interest rate when borrowing money.

- **The base interest rate:** The interest rate the mortgage professional secured from the lender for your mortgage.

- **The Annual Percentage Rate (APR):** The total cost of your loan including the closing costs that are divided over the number of years of your loan. (This number will be different than the base interest rate which does not have any fees or closing costs factored in)

- **The lifetime cost of the loan:** The big scary number that shows you how much you are paying back over the next thirty years.

Here is a chart to further illustrate the point of the impact of interest rates on your mortgage.

Monthly Payments for $250,000 (30 Year Fixed Rate Mortgage)	
This chart shows you how your monthly payment can change based on the interest rate. (Taxes, insurance and other payments not included)	
5.0%	$1,342
5.5%	$1,419
6.0%	$1,498
6.5%	$1,580

7.0%	$1,663
7.5%	$1,748
8.0%	$1,834
8.5%	$1,922
9.0%	$2,011
9.5%	$2,102
10.0%	$2,193

So What is Better, Fixed Or Adjustable?

The best mortgage for you depends on your goals and needs. Only you and your family can make the ultimate decision, but here is a chart to guide you in making your decision.

Mortgage Program Selection Guide	
You should get a fixed interest rate mortgage... (***Includes 30, 25, 20, or 15 year term periods.)	If you: • Want stability • Want peace of mind • Are risk-adverse • Do not know if you will ever get a raise that is more than the rate of inflation • Do not ever want to move again • Have your ultimate dream home • Have a long term plan for the house
You should get an adjustable rate mortgage...	If you: • Plan on moving in the next three to five years

(***Includes 1/1, 2/1, 3/1, 5/1, 7/1, 10/1, Option ARMs, Interest Only ARMs, Hybrid ARMs)	• Make seasonal income that varies dramatically • Do not mind a little risk • Have significant savings • Bought a starter home knowing you will outgrow it quickly • Do not really like the house, but it works for now • Manage your finances well • Have a strong financial markets background and understand how financial markets operate.

The Truth About Points, Fees And Yield Spread

When obtaining a mortgage points, fees and yield spread are terms you should know and understand. They are lumped into three major categories:

- **Mortgage Points** – You may be offered to pay points to get a lower interest rate or you may be charged a point by the mortgage lender for originating your mortgage. If you are paying points to get a lower interest rate, it is called discount points. Points are equal to 1% of your loan amount. So if your mortgage is $250,000 then one point is $2,500.

- **Mortgage Fees** – Fees are the costs that you pay, because you are getting a mortgage. You must be careful in this area, because some mortgage lenders will really pile them on, but generally speaking here are the major ones you should expect to pay:

- **Appraisal**: Lenders require appraisals to determine the home value before they make a lending decision.

- **Attorney Fee/Escrow Fee/Settlement Fee**: Every mortgage closing needs a third party to handle the closing and disperse funds.

- **Credit Report**: Your lender will not make a lending decision without reviewing your credit reports.

- **Courier Fee**: In some cases there are several documents that are required to be shipped overnight.

- **Flood Certification**: Your house must not be in a flood plain and to determine this you must pay a fee.

- **Processing Fee**: Every mortgage has a fair amount of paper work that requires a gatekeeper for completing and submitting paperwork to lenders.

- **Recording Fee or Reconveyance Fee**: In order to make your sale final and legally binding, your mortgage paperwork has to be documented at the courthouse.

- **Tax Service Fee**: Lenders always make sure that your taxes on the house are paid current before you close.

- **Title Insurance**: This one-time fee protects you against other people making a claim that they are the rightful owners of your home. The law requires this.

- **Title Review**: In some cases your attorney will charge a separate fee for reviewing all of the past records for your title.

- *Underwriting Fee:* Every lender charges an underwriting fee to perform all of the necessary evaluations before lending you money.

- **Yield Spread Premium** – It is basically an incentive program paid by your mortgage lender to your mortgage professional for either charging you a higher interest rate or qualifying you for a specific mortgage program. This is one area, which has been under a lot of scrutiny in recent years, because it has caused some loan officers to steer clients towards dangerous mortgage programs as a result of the profit in doing so. Be sure to ask your mortgage professional how many points will he or she be earning total on your mortgage and simply ask for a par rate.

The Best First-Time Home buyer Mortgage Program

There is one mortgage program which allows all qualified applicants to get the lowest fixed interest rate available and take advantage of the best down payment assistance programs. In my experience every first time home buyers should work with a mortgage company that specializes in conventional mortgage and FHA (Federal Housing Administration) mortgages. The FHA is a government agency that insures residential mortgage loans for people who are interested in purchasing their first home – or even their second home after a specified period of time of non-ownership. An FHA loan is designed to help potential homeowners for those buyers who want to minimize their down payment to qualify for a conventional mortgage loan.

When choosing a mortgage lender be sure to find out if you will have access to all of the area mortgage programs or just a few. In most cases your regular bank which holds your savings and checking account can only allow you to use their own programs. Their limited options may or may not work out in your favor.

A FHA mortgage also helps people who have less than perfect credit, build their credit and increase their FICO score. This can help them later down the line secure loans for vehicles, furniture, home improvement projects, and even credit cards. If you pay your mortgage on time every month, your credit score will improve drastically just within the first five years of paying your mortgage. If you are lucky enough to be able to pay off your home early, you will be able to enjoy the extra money for other things, such as a dream vacation, all without worrying about defaulting on your home.

The paperwork and components that you will need to get approved for a FHA mortgage are the same as with a conventional mortgage:

- W2's from the last two tax years
- Last two years of complete tax returns
- Paystubs from last two pay periods
- Previous two months of bank statements
- Two years of stable job history
- Proof of at least 12-24 months of on-time rent payments
- 3 – 5% of purchase price for the down payment
- Basic forms verifying your identity, mortgage loan application and employment history

In this next section I will cover the questions that first-time home buyers should ask their mortgage professional about their mortgage loans. I will also review the major mistakes many new home buyers make during the purchasing process and help dispel some of the myths that surround FHA loans.

Q & A: FHA Mortgages

Once you have placed an offer on a home, placed an earnest money deposit, if required, on the house. Then, the next step is to obtain financing for your home. As a new home buyer, you should be aware of how this process works. These questions and answers will help educate you on the process and how this applies to an FHA loan.

- **What type of guidelines do I have to meet for an FHA loan?**

  Since FHA loans are considered the easiest mortgage loan to qualify for and the most flexible, the guideline you need to meet are not that difficult.

  You must have:

    o At least two years of steady employment preferably with the same employer.
    o Income over the last two years that has been steady or has increased.
    o Less than two thirty-day late payments over the last two years or a letter explaining the issues on the credit report to satisfy the FHA inquiry.
    o If you have filed for bankruptcy in the past, it must be at least two years old with a good credit record since filing.
    o A mortgage payment that equals approximately 30% of your gross income which is based on the purchase price of the house, your other monthly bills, income, and current interest rates.

- **After I fill out the mortgage application, how long do I have wait for an answer?**
  Getting an answer on whether or not you are accepted for the loan you applied for can take anywhere from 24

hours to 15 days. If you are required to provide the loan officer additional documentation – such as an explanation of items on your credit report – this could affect the time it takes to get an answer. The faster you provide the information, the faster you will get an answer. The lender reviewing your application will also be requesting an appraisal of the property, a copy of your credit report, verification of your employment information and banking records.

- **How much do I need for a down payment if I qualify for a FHA loan?**

Most loans require a down payment that equals approximately 3.5% - 10% of the purchasing price. Your mortgage professional will be able to tell you how much you need for a down payment. FHA will allow applicants to use money that is given to them from a family member or employer for their down payment.

- **What will the annual percentage rate on my loan be? Is it the same as the interest rate on my loan?**

The annual percentage rate (APR) is not the same as the interest rate on your loan. The interest rate on your loan is the percentage you pay per so many dollars you borrow. This is the fee the lender charges you to borrow the money.

The APR is a value that reflects the actual cost of borrowing the money and it includes all of the fees that go with purchasing your home. Because each loan is different, your APR will be different than someone else's. There is no set number because the government uses a special formula to calculate this number. This number is determined by taking the amount of money you are borrowing and adding the closing costs on the loan and any other fees accumulated to the borrowing amount. All of the interest that you will be paying over the length of the loan – usually 30 years for an FHA loan – is added into the figure and it is then broken down into the rate, reflected as percentage.

Say you borrow $50,000 to pay for the home. Your closing costs are $700, and additional fees equal $2,000. Your APR will be determined how much interest is paid on $52,700 over 30 years and then broken down into a percentage.

- **What about the interest rate on my loan? Is it locked in place until I close or will it change?**

The interest rate on your loan you received as your initial quote may be different from your final closing, unless you submitted a purchase and sales contract, complete loan application, and property appraisal. The interest rate will fluctuate with the market and most companies can no longer lock a rate into place until they have all of three of these documents on file. If you want to get the lower rate, then you should submit the necessary items as soon as possible.

- **Will I get penalized if I pay off my mortgage loan before the end of the term?**

Usually there is no prepayment penalty, but you should verify this information with your mortgage company after you have secured your loan to be sure. Each lender is a little different so it is better to err on the side of caution and assume nothing. It would be horrible to pay off your home to find out that you still owe the lender, because of a prepayment penalty amount.

- **What could delay the approval of my mortgage loan?**

There are many things that could delay your approval and most of them are usually beyond your control, unless you decide to request specific things that pertain to the property you are purchasing, such as having the home cleaned before moving in, repairs, and other issues.

Top Ten Tricks Dishonest Loan Officers Will Use To Rip You Off

1. Low-ball Offers – The loan officer tells you that you can qualify for an interest rate that is nowhere near what you can actually qualify for. This is just a trick to get you wrapped up and involved before you know what is going on. Get it in writing or it does not exist!

2. Prepayment Penalty – In this day and age there is no reason that anyone should have a prepayment penalty unless you verbally request one. At any rate the choice should be yours to make.

3. Charging loan origination fees AND loan discount fees without lowering the interest rate because of the discount point. They just keep the extra money they make on the deal when in actuality you are paying the discount fee to get a lower interest rate.

4. Charging email and administration fees.

5. Not disclosing their actual compensation on the mortgage.

6. Not releasing your appraisal when you choose to go with another lender.

7. Switching the loan programs the day of closing.

8. Not giving you a Good Faith Estimate.

9. Saying they have access to a special loan program that no one else has.

10. Receiving kickbacks from real estate agents, title companies and appraisers in exchange for referring you to their business.

But I Heard That FHA Mortgages Are...

Anyone who is interested in securing an FHA mortgage for their home may hear a bunch of things about FHA loans that are not necessarily true. There are a ton of false rumors such as, FHA mortgages have difficult requirements to meet, needing perfect credit, and/or having to have a large down payment. Hearing these types of things could make a potential new home buyer nervous about buying a home. In this section I'm going to debunk these myths so that you truly understand how easy it really is to secure one of these versatile loans and get the home of your dreams.

- **Myth #1 – The government loans you the money for your home.**

  The FHA does not loan you money. The FHA simply insures the money that a bank, credit union, or other financial institution loans you. If you default on the mortgage, the FHA pays the lender the money you owe. This is one of the reasons why banks are able to loosen up their requirements for home loans. They are actually taking less of risk on you, because of the government's promise to pay them.

- **Myth #2 – Your credit score does not matter when it comes to an FHA loan.**

  FHA lenders base their decision not only on your FICO or credit score, but on your actual credit history over the last two or more years. The state of your credit history is more important and they are looking for the way you make your payments – on time or late – and patterns of payment. The FHA will also take into consideration utility bill payments, rental history, phone bills, and other monthly bills that can help determine your credit worthiness.

- **Myth #3 – You get a better deal with an FHA loan.**

  This is not always true. Yes, this type of loan carries fewer risks for your lender and you get charged less by them, but they are not always the better deal. The FHA makes their money from the insurance that is paid to them. FHA loans are the better deal if you have low income or bad credit. If you have medium to good credit, you could get a better deal with a conventional mortgage loan. Your mortgage professional can assist in this area further. Ask them for multiple loan choices to choose from.

- **Myth #4 – You will have to wait longer for an FHA loan approval.**

  This is a big, resounding no. Thanks to the Internet, computers allow for automated underwriting and paperless processing, so it does not take the FHA any longer to approve a loan that it does a conventional loan. If you are under the care of an FHA educated loan officer, the process could even go faster as the paperwork and any documentation needed is submitted all at once instead of piecemeal.

- **Myth #5 – There is a ton of extra paperwork associated with an FHA loan.**

  This is another big resounding no. Conventional loans and FHA loans have pretty much the same amount of paperwork that needs to be filled out and submitted. The FHA loans do require a few different, extra documents that need to be filled out, but they are designed to protect you while you are going through the process of securing the loan. Plus, with the ability to print off most of the documents with your demographic information – address, phone number, income, etc. – already filled in, the most you will need to do is initial a few more pages.

- **Myth #6 – I'm going to pay more for a FHA loan than a conventional one.**

  I'm not sure how this particular myth got started, but the interest rate that is used on a conventional loan is the same that is used on an FHA loan. Both are based on the current market factors and interest rates that are in force at the time of price locking. As a matter of fact, most of the time the FHA mortgage payment is less expensive than a conventional loan. First time buyers with an FHA loan actually make out better because their FICO score is not used to base interest rates on. Even with the FHA insurance premium rolled into the loan, the monthly amount could be less.

- **Myth #7 – The FHA mortgage insurance is unaffordable.**

  Not really. Any loan in which 80% or more of the property value is financed must carry mortgage insurance, whether it is a conventional loan or a FHA loan. This is in place so that a portion of the loan is paid to the lender if the borrower defaults on their payments. The previous rule stated that that all buyers had to pay 20% down in order to get a mortgage. This is no longer the case.

- **Myth #8 – The guidelines for an FHA loan is very restrictive.**

  Once again, the answer here is no. FHA loans are actually very easy on borrowers. They have a higher maximum loan amount and they do not require an income restriction, like Fannie Mae and Freddie Mac loans, two companies that specialize in conventional loans. Buyers with credit history issues will find an FHA loan easier to obtain. Plus FHA loans allow underwriters to actually look at the loan application and use common sense techniques to help decide whether or not you can actually afford and pay your mortgage. FHA loans also allow for a no re-qualifying refinance process if the interest rates should drop drastically, allowing borrowers to refinance for a lower monthly payment.

Choosing a Mortgage Professional

After many years of counseling home buyers through some very rough waters with other mortgage professionals, I'm convinced there is only one smart way to find a mortgage professional.

- One of the above should be a referral from a friend, family member or co-worker that has worked with the mortgage professional.
- Ask for a specific person to work with.

My reasoning is simple. You should not be talking to a mystery voice on the phone during the most exciting yet stressful financial decision of your life. You need someone you can see face to face when things get rough. Someone you can locate easily whenever you have a question. More importantly, you need someone you can trust.

What you should **NOT** do is:

- **Call around for rate quotes** - There are some loan officers who will give you a low-ball rate that they cannot possibly follow through on. This is just a deceptive plot to get your business.

- **Compare annual percentage rates** - Many lenders use several different factors to come up with APR. Very rarely do two banks use the same formula.

- **Compare ads** - The ads are to get you into the office to sign up. Mortgage companies put the most attractive information that applies for less than 1% of the population to bait and switch you.

The reason why you should not use those three methods is because they leave too much wiggle room for unscrupulous loan officers to trick you into giving your information, which leads us right into...

The next step to take once you find a good mortgage professional is to interview him or her using questions like:

- Are you a mortgage broker, banker or direct lender?
- Are you licensed by the state and have any complaints ever been filed against you?
- Is the interest rate you quoted me fixed or adjustable?
- Are you locking in the interest rate and if so then for how long?
- What is your fee for doing the mortgage?
- What additional fees will be added to the mortgage besides yours?
- What will be the total principal amount of the loan?
- How much will my monthly payments be?
- What is the length of the loan?
- Will my loan be sold?
- Will I have a prepayment penalty?
- If I pay for the appraisal will you immediately give me a copy of it when you receive it?
- If I pay for the credit report will you immediately give me a copy of it?
- Who do I contact to get a copy of the closing documents 24 hours before closing?
- How long will it take to get me an approval?

7 Reasons Why You Should Work With Your Local Mortgage Professional Or Risk Disaster

1. You can meet face to face to interview your local mortgage professional.

2. You can talk to the local mortgage professional face to face if there is a problem.

3. Your local mortgage professional can attend the closing and help with any errors that show up last minute.

4. Your local mortgage professional will be familiar with local real estate market trends.

5. Your local mortgage professional will have relationships with the attorney and title company actually performing your closing.

6. Your local mortgage professional will know the standard local fees that are charged.

7. Your local mortgage professional is more likely to have a visible and easily reachable team to help out during the process.

Applying For Your Mortgage

When you are meeting with your mortgage professional, you should come prepared. I have seen it take weeks for some buyers to get their paperwork together for an appointment and I have seen other people do it in minutes. Generally speaking, here is the information you want to bring to your appointment:

*   W2's from the last two tax years
*   Last two years of complete tax returns
*   Two most recent paystubs

- Previous two months of bank statements
- Rent payment receipts for the last 12 months
- Proof that you have the 3.5 – 10% of purchase price for the down payment
- Basic forms that verify your identity and employment history

Once your mortgage professional has this information in hand, you will receive your prequalification letter and a Good Faith Estimate. The Good Faith Estimate is a form that gives you all of fees and information about your mortgage. Keep in mind that it is an estimate, but it should be within 10% of the final numbers for your mortgage.

The Four Factors Of Getting Your Mortgage Approvals Fast And Easy

There are four major factors that will determine your mortgage approval and the interest rate you will be paying.

1. **Income** – Have you had continuous employment for the last twenty-four months and if so, how much have you averaged per hour? Remember to keep your base salary separate from over-time and bonuses, because lenders view those two numbers very differently as they are not stable and reliable enough to merit the same weight as salary.

   - *High Income Earners* - Just because you make $150,000 per year does not mean you are not hourly. Take a look at your paystub and you will find that your employer graciously took the time to break it down for you.

   - *Self-Employed* – All the hard work you and your tax professional put into minimizing your tax liability could really hurt you. Here is why: lenders look at your net income for the tax year not your gross income. Meaning if your half a million dollar a year business deducted every possible penny you could and only showed you with a net of twenty five thousand dollars for the tax year, then that is all lenders can use to qualify you for a mortgage. A paltry twenty five thousand dollars. I know...I know, it is not right, but that is the way it is in Mortgageville.

2. **Credit** – Does your credit reports reflect steady payment history and the ability to manage your finances or does it show a person who rarely pays bills on time?

3. **Loan-To-Value (LTV)** – Are you looking to essentially finance every single penny that you can or are you putting a sizable down payment? Lenders are limiting their financing to about 97% for first-time home buyers in the current economy. If the purchase price is $250,000 and you have $7,500 for a down payment and closing costs, then you are borrowing $242,500. That means that you have a 97% LTV.

EXAMPLE:

$250,000 purchase price - $7,500 down payment = $242,500
$242,500 / $250,000 = .97 or 97% LTV

4. **Rental Payment History** – Can you prove you have been paying your rent on time that last twenty-four months? This can be easily shown by receipts and check stubs.

Why You May Get A Different Interest Rate Than The Advertisement Says

Over the years, there have been many times when home buyers have become upset, because they were promised a 4.99% interest rate from another mortgage professional who couldn't deliver on his promise. When I dug a little deeper, I discovered that the interest rate they "thought" they were getting was actually an advertisement in the newspaper, and it did not accurately reflect their true income, credit and overall risk level from a lender's perspective.

So, here are some of the occasions in which you might find yourself getting a dramatically different interest rate than what you heard on the radio, saw on T.V. or read in the newspaper.

- **You chose a different mortgage type.** Many times lenders will put the most attractive rates in their ads. However, they neglect to mention less than one percent of the population qualifies for these programs.

- **On paper you look risky.** There is no substitute for having good credit and consistent income. If you do not have either then you may have a good story to tell, but on paper you look risky.

- **You are almost borrowing what the house is worth (High LTV).** Since the days of one hundred percent financing are mostly gone, most buyers are only putting down 3%-5%, which means that you are financing 97% - 95% of the property value. This usually results in a higher interest rate.

- **Your loan cannot be resold on the secondary market.** Banks view mortgages as investments so they will package ten or twenty mortgages together and sell them as an investment package to other banks. So, if they have a group of ten thirty year fixed mortgages with six percent interest rates they will expect a six percent return each year for thirty years. However, if you are viewed as risky then they might not be able to sell your mortgage to other investors and so you represent more risk to them.

- **Your loan may or may not have points.** The mortgage rate you saw may have included paying one or two points. However, if you stated you did not want to pay points to your mortgage professional, then you may get a higher interest rate and points. The points are included in the interest rate in order to provide compensation to the mortgage professional. This is otherwise called yield spread premium.

Qualifying For A Super-Size Jumbo Mortgage

Here is a news flash for you in case you hadn't noticed. In many areas the price of a home is well above the old $417,000 conventional loan limits! This could potentially add another level of stress to first-time home buyers who are preparing to jump into this part of the market. However, don't worry because I have put together a guide to walk you through the differences and what to expect when you need a lot more than $417,000 to buy your home:

- **Expect to pay a slightly higher interest rate.** You have to be prepared to ignore those annoying advertisement commercials that promise you 3.99% interest rates on a million dollar mortgage. They are simply not true for the majority of borrowers.

- **Be prepared for additional time to close.** Lenders usually have more questions and need more careful market analysis when lending on luxury homes. They're not just picking on you. It is because luxury homes usually take longer to sell.

- **You may be asked for additional income documentation.** This is not the time to play vague mystery person with rich relatives. Lenders want to know who, when, why and where your money and income comes from.

- **Your credit reports will be more closely scrutinized.** Due to the mortgage amount, any little blemish on your credit could become a blaring issue in light of trying to borrow a jumbo amount of money.

- **Be willing, ready and able to talk about where your money comes from and why you get paid the way you do.** It is very likely that if you are seriously considering a jumbo mortgage, then you make jumbo-like income. With that being said it is even more important that you be open, honest and forthcoming about every source of income reflecting on your tax returns.

- **Get out the checkbook because the appraisal and home inspection will cost considerably more than average homes.** Be prepared to pay slightly higher prices for your real estate services because of the risk involved with doing a larger mortgage.

Smart Home Buyer Program
Step #6

1. Find at least three neighborhoods which fit your criteria and do online research, drive-bys and meet the locals to learn:

    - Who the neighbors are
    - Crime rates
    - School system options
    - Hidden houses for sale

2. Write down the addresses of houses for sale. Go to an online real valuation service and look up houses that were sold in the last six months. Make sure the houses are similar to the prospective house and within three miles of the house.

Smart Home Buyer Program
Step #7

1. Complete the five-step formula for finding and
    maximizing down payment programs.

2. Determine if you will use your savings,
    investments or if you need to ask family or friends
    for assistance.

What is Coming Up Next ...

Having your down payment money taken care of gives
you an extra bit of relief; however when you combine that
with the tips and strategies I present to you in the next
chapter on mortgages you will be able to save thousands
of dollars and prevent yourself from being ripped off.

CHAPTER 7

Pros & Cons to Down Payment Assistance
Things You Must Consider Before Using Down Payment Assistance & First Time Buyer Programs

Over the years I have had many happy surprises, but few have matched the joys of receiving free money. I know, I know. It sounds shallow. However, I'm sure that if someone walked up to you right now and handed you an envelope stuffed with cash, you would smile from ear to ear.

Well, that is what this chapter does. I'll take you by the hand and walk you into your own private little bank vault. You can stroll right in and grab fists full of cash and happily be on your way. We will start with going over the basics and then I will walk you right through the strategies that are the keys to the bank.

Down Payment Assistance Program Basics

As with most things in life there are some ground rules for gaining access to the hidden cash you will need for your down payment. However, there is no need to be too alarmed because the rules are pretty simple and many first-time home buyers easily qualify, but first we will start with the definition of down payment assistance.

Down payment assistance is any form of money you receive

from an organization, company, family member or friend that you can use to pay your closing costs and down payment requirement on your home. Yes, I consider money from anyone else outside of your household to be down payment assistance. So I will cover those topics as well so that you can protect yourself, your friend or family member from tax hits or disagreements later on. Learn how to take advantage of down payment assistance whether it be from traditional programs or from your personal resources. Down payment assistance sometimes can help not only you but also help those that gift or loan you the assistance.

Standard Down Payment Assistance Guidelines

In order for you to qualify for most down payment assistance programs, usually you must be a first-time home buyer. Most of the guidelines to qualify for the programs are simple; however there are some programs that have a few more requirements. It is also important for you to know that the real estate definition of first-time home buyer does not actually mean a "first time" home buyer. It usually means you meet the following guidelines:

- **You have not owned a property in the last 3 years.** – This is a rule to protect the best down payment money programs from being abused by people who are only buying houses to resale them for a quick profit.

- **You have not purchased Real Estate in the state you are looking to purchase now.-** Some states consider first time home buying on a state to state basis.

- **You do not own any other real estate property.** – This includes any real estate property where you are on the title or on the mortgage. Yes, this means timeshares where you have an ownership stake on the title.

- **Your income meets the guidelines.** – Most down

payment assistance programs were created for low to middle income families.

- **You meet the credit guidelines.** – Yes, the best down payment programs still require you to show that you can manage your debts responsibly. The minimum credit score is determined by your mortgage lender. The good news is that when you are approved for the mortgage, often your chances of getting approved for the down payment assistance programs increases greatly.

- **The home purchase price meets the lenders guidelines.** – The home purchase price is usually limited to the conforming mortgage limits for a single family house or the Federal Housing Agency (FHA) limit set for a single family house. However, there are programs that also allow you to purchase a multi-family home.

- **The prospective home is in the right geographic area.** – Many down payment assistance programs are designed to promote homeownership in targeted areas. Keep in mind that the target areas also determine exactly how much assistance you can receive. You can learn the specific target areas by reviewing the program guidelines.

- **The type of house you buy.** – You usually have flexibility for up to a four-unit home, but the majority of down payment assistance programs will limit you to a single-family home.

- **The type of mortgage program you receive.** – It is important that you know that many of the best down payment assistance programs usually require you to use a FHA mortgage. The reason for this trend is because the FHA insures the mortgages, so in the event that you do not make the payment the lender will still get paid.

Are we there yet?...Are we there yet?...Are we there...

Karl and Maria were frugal by nature, but coming up with the down payment money was taking longer than they planned. First of all, Karl had taken a huge loss in his 401k retirement plan and his company put a freeze on the plan to protect their employee's money. This was a huge hit to their plans.

Secondly, Maria was three months pregnant and wanted to get moved in and "situated" before the baby came. She also did not want to completely drain their savings right before they welcomed their first child into the world.

This left them in a tough situation. It was Maria who first suggested spending the bulk of their time looking for a down payment assistance program before going nuts driving around every weekend looking at house after house. It was not long before she came across a great online resource, which revealed all of the down payment programs in their town. She squealed in delight.

Two weeks later they secured over fifteen thousand dollars in down payment assistance money and were able to seriously think about closing on a home in six weeks.

You will be happy to know they have a healthy baby boy in their brand new home.

How To Find And Maximize The Best Government Sponsored Down Payment Assistance Programs

The Federal and local governments have done a tremendous amount to ease the financial burden of first-time home buyer down payments. These programs are usually administered by the U.S Department of Housing and Urban Development (HUD) in order to provide uniform qualifying guidelines. The local and federal government programs, designed to help home buyers, usually take the shape of lower interest rates on the first and second mortgages, down payment assistance loans or grants to assist in paying for closing costs and down payments.

The process to qualify for these programs usually mirrors that of the mortgage process, so it should seem very familiar and go hand in hand with qualifying for your first mortgage. In my opinion, even if it were a little different, you should be okay with doing a little more paperwork to get upwards of $15,000 or $20,000 in zero percent interest on a down payment to buy your home.

I think you will be glad to know that there is a specific strategy to use to find your down payment assistance programs. I will reveal my four-step formula to help you come up with the cash to buy your home.

Step 1: Review Your Home Dream List

Reviewing your Dream Home List allows you to focus on one particular house type and area. This is a vital first step because every town, city and even neighborhood may have a different down payment assistance program. It is important that you target all of your attention to the area you desire to live in. Here are two important things that you want to pay attention to:

- **House Type** – You need to know if you want a single family, multi-family, condo or townhouse. Each one of these housing types have different rules and guidelines when it comes to mortgages and down payment assistance programs.

- **Geographic Location** – Every down payment assistance program has a target geographic area. Sometimes it is a city or town, but many times it could be as specific as a neighborhood.

Step 2: Review Your Housing Cash Flow Sheet

You need to know your expected yearly income before applying for down payment assistance programs. Many programs have income limitations that could easily eliminate most high income earners from qualifying. Here is how you can get an estimate of your yearly income:

- **Current Estimated Income** – Take your monthly income from your cash flow worksheet and multiply it by twelve. This will allow you to know if you would exceed the income levels. Remember to also do the calculation for anyone else who would be applying with you.

Step 3: How To Determine How Much Down Payment Money You will Need

If you have been saving up for your home for the last several years, then you already know how much you have put aside for your down payment. Additionally, if you do not have anything saved up, then it is also easy to know how much you have put aside. However if you are somewhere in the middle, meaning you have some savings, like a 401k and a couple of investments, then you will need to do some math in regards to what you want to contribute.

Regardless of your savings *or* lack of savings, what you need to know at this stage is how much you will be required to contribute for the down payment as required by your mortgage lender. The mortgage program you will be using usually determines this. At this stage, you may not know your mortgage program, so simply use five percent of your target home price.

For example: $200,000 sales price x 5% = $10,000

Step 4: Putting It All Together

Now it is time to put the pieces together. Here is what you need to do:

- **Organize your information** - You will need a blank sheet of paper to keep your notes for this step. At the top of the page you should write down your target house type, location, yearly income and down payment amount you need.

- **Searching town or city websites** – Go online to your target city's website and search for the "planning and zoning", "housing authority" or "grants" section of the website. Most websites have a sitemap link or search the website function which allows you to type in the search terms and quickly find what you are searching for.

- **Calling the town & city housing departments** – Once you find the section that covers housing or planning and zoning, then write down the contact phone number for that department. Pick up the phone and call them and say the following, "Who can I speak to about home buyer assistance or down payment assistance programs for the town or city?" The person on the other end will either answer with the programs and information or they will give you contact information for someone to speak to.

Do you live here?

When you call the specific town and ask about the down payment programs, be sure to let the person on the other end of the phone know exactly where you want to live. You would be surprised how dramatically some programs vary from neighborhood to neighborhood.

When you are on the phone with the person who is telling you about the down payment assistance programs it is very important that you ask some basic questions. Make sure that you get their name, direct phone number, and email address. You also want to ask them to email you the program guidelines and information as soon as possible. Here is what you will want to ask while on the phone or find the answers to when they email over the program information:

- **What type of mortgage must I use to qualify for this program?** – Every down payment assistance program has restrictions on the type of mortgage program you can use. You simply ask the person what mortgage program you would need to use to qualify for this program.

- **What are the terms, limits and conditions of this program?** – There are some programs that do not require payments or forgive a certain percentage of your down payment assistance for each year you live in the home. The most important limit is the amount of the down payment assistance that you can receive. The usual range is five thousand dollars up to forty thousand dollars. Be sure to ask for any and all conditions in writing if at all possible.

- **Do I have to use a certain mortgage lender for this program?** – Over the years, I have run into down payment assistance programs that require home buyers to use a specific mortgage company, so be sure to ask this question.

How To Find Down Payment Assistance When You Do Not Qualify For The Government Programs

Well if that is you, you are in luck, because there are a couple of ways to come up with the down payment money when you do not qualify for the traditional programs. The best and most recommended way to come up with the funds is to tap your network of friends and family for a gift or loan.

Just so you know what everyone else does when they are faced with this situation, here are traditional places that most people use to pay for their down payment:

- Your 401k

- Your IRA

- Borrow from friends and family

- Down payment gift money from friends and family

- Downsize upcoming events, such as a wedding, and use the difference you save

- Your current savings

Gift Money From Family And Friends

If you find yourself thinking about asking friends and family for financial help with your down payment, you are not alone. According to the National Association of Realtors, about 25% of first-time home buyers get some form of financial assistance from family and friends. Actually they are the best source of help when buying a home because unlike a lender family and friends will also be there to help you with the brand new responsibilities of homeownership.

When you are first contemplating approaching family or friends for financial assistance it is best to be prepared with your mortgage prequalification letter and a standard letter explaining what the money will be used for; called a gift letter. The mortgage prequalification letter answers any asked or unasked questions regarding the legitimacy of your intent to use the money for a home as well as details exactly how much you will need to come up with to close. The gift letter outlines exactly where the funds will be going.

The Necessity of The Gift Letter

There is also a second and more important reason to have a properly worded and structured gift letter. Your mortgage lender will require written documentation to verify many key factors of the down payment gift you are receiving such as:

- The amount of the gift money.

- Your relationship to the gift giver.

- The address and contact information of the gift giver.

- Exact wording stating the money you are receiving is NOT a loan and does not have to be repaid.

If the funds stay in the giver's bank account or possession until the closing date, then you must also take the time to let your gift giver know that they will have to provide:

3. Account holder's financial institution

4. Account number

5. Written authorization to give the mortgage lender permission to contact financial institution to verify the gift

I have a word of caution when you are going the family gift route. Both you and the gift giver should sit down and choose whether or not to disclose to other family members exactly what is going on. This is the best way to avoid issues and interpersonal conflicts that sometimes cause family rifts.
When receiving gift money from your friends or family properly document the gift with your gift letter.

Borrowing Down Payment Funds From Family And Friends

If you do not have family or friends who will gift you the needed money to buy your home, then you may want to consider borrowing the money from them to purchase your home. When your family, friends or any other non-bank party loans you money they are considered a private lender. You may be thinking why would your family or friends want to loan you the money to purchase your home. However, you may be surprised because there are some very significant benefits personal lenders may enjoy such as:

- **Better return rates than banks** – Take a few minutes to shop online for return rates at your local bank and you will quickly see money markets and certificates of deposits are not paying four, five or six percent returns on your money when you invest with them. A private lender will get a better return on each dollar when loaning to you than they would get by keeping their money at a bank.

- **Residual passive income** – By lending you the money, your private lender will receive monthly payments each month as opposed to the occasional payout from regular investments.

- **Lower risk when you know the borrowers personally** – Your private lender can rest a little easier since they know you personally. If they are willing to consider loaning you the money, then you have most likely built up some level of trust. Secondly, they also have the reassurance of having the home as collateral if it ever comes to the point that you have to sell the home to make good on the loan.

- **Feeling good for helping someone they love** – The bond of friendship and parental love often times inspires those around you to desire to help you get ahead in life. Sometimes it is equally as important that loved ones have a chance to help you out as it is for you to be helped.

The Benefits You Receive From Borrowing From Family And Friends

There are also some very attractive reasons for you to borrow from people you know and love such as:

- **Lower interest rates and tax deductions** – It is common for family and friends to loan you money for one to two percent lower than a traditional financial institution. This equates to tens of thousands of dollars over the life of your loan. Additionally, when you properly document the loan you can also realize mortgage interest deductions.

- **Very flexible repayments plans** – A traditional financial institution will never allow you to take several months off from making payments or agree to allow you to make quarterly payments. However, with a private lender, your life situation may require you to ask for some additional flexibility, which has a chance of being permitted.

- **Zero loan fees or points** – It is very unusual for family and friends to charge you anything for coordinating the loan. They usually are very happy with their five or six percent return each month.

- **Flexible guidelines to qualify** – Your private loan approval is simply based on how well the family member or friend trusts you.   There is no requirement for outstanding credit scores.

- **Possibly no private mortgage insurance** – If you have a generous lender who will allow you to borrow more than 20% of your purchase price then you can avoid the often times annoying Private Mortgage Insurance (PMI) which can equate to thousands of dollars in savings each year.

- **No long drawn out approval process** – There are no loan underwriters, loan officers, quality control inspectors or anyone else except you and the private lender to understand and agree to the terms of the loan.

You Need How Much For What?

There are few things, which are more uncomfortable than asking for money from a family member or friend; however it is much easier when you are prepared with the relevant information such as:

- **How much you need to borrow** – Try to be as specific and accurate as possible because it is very difficult to return back and ask for more money.

- **The specific interest rate you will be paying back** – As a general rule of thumb, the higher the interest rate you are paying back, the better it is viewed.

- **Your repayment schedule** – This would be your timetable to pay the money back over a period of time.

- **The amount of money you are contributing to the down payment** – If you are putting in ten thousand dollars of your own money it might make the other party more comfortable knowing you have skin in the game.

- **Information about how strong your financial ability is to repay the loan** – This could be the length of time at a job, your two most recent paystubs and last year's W2's.

- **What type of financial security you offer the lender** – Talk about the fact that you have disability insurance or unemployment insurance which covers the amount of your monthly payment.

- **The monetary benefits to the lender** – Do not assume that the other party realizes how much of a return they will get for loaning you the money. Discuss how much they'll make over the life of the loan to you.

The Interest Rate Police

When using a private loan your lender may really want to give you a great deal by offering a very low interest rate. In theory it is a no-brainer, but when it comes to the IRS it is a no-no. Sure your private lender has every right to charge you anything from 0% up to the legal limit in your state, however there are some watchdogs at the Federal level.

Your loan interest rate can be lower than a traditional financial lender's rate, but it must be higher than what is known as the Applicable Federal Rate (AFR). The AFR is the minimum interest rate that a lender can charge for lending you money. The reason the IRS sets this interest rate is to limit the amount of money that is loaned out at below market rates for the purpose of avoiding paying taxes. If your private lender gives an interest rate that is below the AFR, then the private lender will be taxed and the minimum interest rate set on the date of the execution of the loan agreement. The best way to find out the going rate for borrowing and lending money is to visit www.irs.gov to learn the AFR and then require your private lender to charge you at least the minimum interest rate.

Putting Your Loan Package Together

While you will want to sit and talk about your loan request with your private lender, you will definitely be required to have the loan agreement in writing to make the contract legally enforceable. And unless you are a real estate attorney, you may be clueless when it comes to drawing up legally binding real estate contracts. You will also want to turn to your real estate attorney for a couple of other reasons. For example, if you are unable to meet your monthly obligation and your primary mortgage holder forecloses on the house in order to sell to recoup their money, then your private lender will not be considered as a lien holder on the property. Secondly, you will need to have a legally binding and compliant document to get your tax deduction.

The two documents that make your loan package legally binding are:

Promissory note – This is a document that states the

amount, interest rate, repayment schedule and all other terms and conditions of the loan.

- **Mortgage** – You may be able to avoid the mortgage document if your loan is a small amount of money, but I personally advise against proceeding without it because it protects you and your private lender in worst-case financial emergencies.

The Joys Of Seller Financing

Believe it or not, there are times when the seller will act as your mortgage lender. The seller does this by providing you with a lump sum of money in the form of a second mortgage or even your entire mortgage doing what is called a "seller-held second" or "seller carry back." In some cities these types of options have become increasingly more popular. Incredulous as this may sound, there are some very legitimate reasons why the seller would extend this great benefit to you such as when:

- It is difficult to sell a home because the market is slow or the home needs some work.

- The house has a lot of built up equity and the seller does not want to take the tax hit all at once when selling so by accepting monthly payments the tax liability is decreased.

- The seller can sell for a higher asking price by having flexible loan terms.

- The seller wants a steady income stream to supplement retirement income instead of receiving a lump sum of cash all at once.

Whatever the reason the seller offers financing, you should be prepared to take advantage of the offer when needed, but also be prepared to give up some negotiating power, because the seller knows you most likely need their financing. In most cases, the length of time you should expect from the seller to repay the loan will be anywhere from three to five years. At the end of the term you will be expected to pay off the balance of the loan by refinancing with a traditional mortgage lender. This is defined as a balloon payment because of the large lump sum, which is due at the end of the loan term.

In return for giving up some negotiating terms in exchange for seller financing you may also want to ask for:

1. No early prepayment penalty when you refinance or pay off the loan early.

2. Lower monthly payments in the beginning, because you will have a balloon payment at the end of the loan term.

3. Lower interest rate, because it is seller financing.

4. Longer time length before the balloon payment is due, preferably five to seven years.

5. Flexibility to transfer the second mortgage to a qualified buyer in the event you sell your home before the loan term is up. This is referred to as assuming the mortgage.

Smart Home Buyer Program
Step #7

- Complete the five-step formula for finding and maximizing down payment programs.

- Determine if you will use your savings, investments or if you need to ask family or friends for assistance.

What is Coming Up Next ...

Having your down payment money taken care of gives you an extra bit of relief. However, when you combine that with the tips and strategies I present to you in the next chapter on mortgages, you will be able to save thousands of dollars and prevent yourself from being ripped off.

CHAPTER 8

Finding Hidden Gems in Unfamiliar Areas
Evaluating the Aspects & Amenities of
Communities to Identify Possible Areas

I n this marvelous age of technology, it is possible to get a great feeling of a real estate market without ever leaving your bedroom. You can gain valuable insight by "surfing the net" which will enable you to recognize a good deal when you see one and avoid the lemons. Thanks to the Internet, you never have to leave your apartment to find your first home.

In this chapter, I will show you how to peel back the layers of the onion on any real estate market. The way to do this is to examine a real estate market at the local neighborhood level. By following my steps you will get the real story that many real estate agents would be too afraid to tell you.

I will also give you the tools and knowledge for a quick and easy way to evaluate the market no matter where you decide to buy your home. You will receive detailed methods on evaluating a prospective neighborhood using some of my time-tested principals.

Look Out Below...

There's nothing that'll turn your dream house into a nightmare quicker than finding out you overpaid by thirty thousand dollars. You are more likely to make this type of mistake if you are trying to also find your dream home while researching what the market is doing. Focus on learning the market first.

Uncovering Your Ideal Neighborhood

Once you have focused in on a city or town which matches your down payment requirements, then the next step is find the ideal neighborhood for your wants and needs. Here are great starting places to get some insight into prospective areas and neighborhoods.

- **Ask your friends, family and co-workers questions about their home and neighborhood.** They will usually be more than willing to talk with you and share their insights on their likes and dislikes about their neighborhoods.

- **If you are from out of town then you could network with some of the people at your job.** Your new employer may be a treasure chest of information about a prospective new area and they have a vested interest in you acclimating quickly and adjusting to your new life.

- **Look up a real estate agent and call for basic area information.** The agent you select may or may not be your ultimate choice for your real estate agent, but by the nature of their profession a real estate agent will be more than willing to talk to you about potential neighborhoods, in hope of winning your business.

- **Visit the town or city websites and online travel guides for each city.** No matter how long you have lived in a certain city or town there are usually many places that you do not know about and even if you think that you know every place, ask anyway. City and towns are always growing, expanding and changing.

Find Out Who Lives In The Neighborhood

One of the most difficult features to research when looking for a home is the character and composition of a prospective neighborhood. However, if you ask any homeowner what they really like most or hate most about buying their current home, many will tell you it is the neighborhood. Here are some great online resources to get you started:

- **www.google.com** – Type in the name of the prospective neighborhood and scroll through the first couple of pages to see if there is any negative or positive feedback regarding the area. You might be surprised to find some unhappy neighborhood association member has started a blog, which conveniently lists the negative aspects of a particular neighborhood. However, take any findings with a grain of salt.

- **www.mybestsegments.com** – This website gives you a breakdown of the type of people who live in a certain geographic area by zip code. It will give you some pretty cool and neat generalizations, which could include descriptions like "Park Bench Seniors" or "Family Thrifts." Go to the website and click on the button that says "Zip Code Look-Up" and it will let you know the demographics of your target zip code.

- **neighborhoods.realtor.com** – When you visit this website you get an in-depth look at the neighborhood demographics, settings & lifestyle, crime statistics and much more. You will even see houses for sale in the neighborhood, which might interest you.

- **www.bestplaces.net** – This site gives you some detailed information about the political views, religious affiliations and the cost of living of the zip code you enter into its database. This website is a great source of little known information which you may not be able to find anywhere else.

- **www.epodunk.com** – This website provides an encyclopedia-like listing of each town which includes;

history, art, music, events as well as cultural and lifestyle information about each town.

The Neighbors From Hell...Literally

Even before the incident happened, Scott and Karen had always known they were a little more conservative than most folks in **(insert your target neighborhood or town here)**.

They just had no idea that a short eighteen months after buying their new home they'd be begging the neighborhood association to have their neighbors rights revoked. After all, both Scott and Karen were only thirty-two years old and were the "newbies."

It all started when dead animals began to turn up in their back yard. Mysteriously, they were always located on the left side of the yard. It quickly escalated to patches of their lawn grass being turned yellow overnight.

It was not long before Karen pointed the finger at the couple that lived next door. Their neighbors were the only people who seemed to have a Halloween party year-round. It seemed as though their neighbors were real life vampires who gained super powers when night time came.

The worst part was that after the fact and with minimal effort and research Scott found tons of complaints lodged against the strange neighbors over the years.

Thankfully, Karen's uncle was a **(insert your target neighborhood or town here)** police captain and quickly began doing around the clock patrols. It was not too much later that the neighbors sold their house and moved out. Scott just wished they had done their research before going through two years of living hell.

Verifying Neighborhood Safety

As a new homeowner you want to make absolutely sure your new neighborhood is as safe as can be. The ONLY way to tell how safe an area truly is requires you to visit or call the local police station.

You can ask the policeman for their number of reported crime events in the last twelve to twenty-four months in your selected area. You should also ask if they are noticing any alarming trends that you should be worried about. In all my years of real estate investing I have found this to be the number one most effective way to judge whether an neighborhood is safe or not.

Check The Local Neighborhood Zoning

There are few bigger surprises a new homeowner will encounter than learning that a mega-shopping center is in the works next door to their new home. Or worse yet, imagine waiting five years to buy the boat you have always wanted, only to learn you are not permitted to park it in your driveway. Which means you will have to pay some outrageous fees just to have somewhere to store your boat.

Most planning and zoning offices can be found online within minutes. Once you find the contact information you can look over their five or ten year projections. You can also stop into the office and get brochures or free copies of the map of proposed economic development. Armed with these tools you will have significantly more information than most of the current residents of your prospective neighborhood.

You can avoid many days of headaches by learning zoning ordinances prior to buying a home. Here are some of the potential issues that may cause you to violate your local zoning code when you unknowingly do things like:

- Chop down a tree
- Park a large vehicle, RV or boat in your driveway
- Remodel your house
- Start a home-based business
- Add a pool, fence, or a kid's tree house

- Own farm animals

Drive-By Inspections

You can gain valuable insight about a neighborhood by driving through it at various times of day and night. There have been many new homeowners who say they were attracted or deterred from buying a home, because of unusual observations they made while driving around looking for desirable neighborhoods to live in.

The best way to start is to circle potential neighborhoods on your map and then take a drive during all times of day and night at random. Or you can develop your own little pattern to get the most insight. No matter what method you use, be sure to take notes on what you like and did not like on your tour. As you are driving be sure to ask yourself questions like:

- Are there people loitering around doing nothing?
- Are the businesses that I see companies I'm proud and happy to have as my neighbors?
- What is the flow of traffic like?
- Do the owners take care of their homes?
- Are there too many "For Sale" signs here, which could indicate a hot market or people trying to get the heck out of dodge?

Talking To The Locals

If you ever want to know the real deal on a home or neighborhood then spend a couple of hours walking through the neighborhood and talking to the neighbors. You will get an earful about local politics, ordinances that everyone hates and juicy gossip about who is doing what and with whom. Peppered throughout the news you will receive, you will also get some great gems and nuggets that can be useful in determining if the neighborhood is best suited towards your needs.

When walking through the neighborhoods look for people outside playing with their kids, walking their pets or simply out washing the car or gardening. You can start up a conversation by being honest and polite about what you are doing and then proceed with several of the following questions:

- Are you happy living in this neighborhood?
- If you could change one thing about this area, what would it be?
- Which streets do you consider to be too busy for kids?
- Do you feel safe walking outside at nighttime?
- Who do you think would be a good fit for this neighborhood?

Those are just a few of the questions you should be asking, but there are many more that we cover in detail in upcoming chapters.

The Convenience Factor: How Close Are You To "Everything Else?"

If you are like other home buyers, then you will also want to know where the local shopping plazas, churches, schools, parks and local "spots" are located. It is hard to imagine a full life without all of the creature comforts that make us glad to be American.

An easy way to find out is to visit **www.homepages.com** and locate any establishment or service provider you are looking for. The next step is to go to **www.mapquest.com** and put in the address from your prospective home or neighborhood. That will give you a good idea of the commute time for any one of your desired destinations.

However, the best method to finding out how convenient places of interest, fun and business are to your potential home is by getting in your car and going for a little drive. Yes, that is right. The good old-fashioned method of driving around and looking out the window is the surest and most dependable way to learn if you can get to a grocery store within ten minutes for your favorite late night snack.

Where Are All The Good Schools?

As a parent or parent-to-be your child's education is always at the forefront of your mind. There are few things that get parents blood boiling more than an ineffective school system. Education is very important when it comes to families.

Even if you do not plan on having children you still want to know what the educational system is like in your neighborhood so when the time comes to sell your home you have a great base of desirable attributes to pull from. Here are some of the online resources that will give you a great snapshot of the neighborhood's school system:

- *www.schoolmatters.com* – This website is a great source of school demographics overall student performance for schools.

- *www.greatschools.net* – This site gives you a side-by-side comparison of schools as well as tools to research a specific school based on the input of parents who have rated the schools.

- The local board of education website and resources should also provide information which you may find helpful and useful in your research. You may also want to consider visiting one of the schools on an open house night to get a better feel.

Finding Houses For Sale In Your Desired Neighborhood

Okay so you have done your neighborhood homework and you have a few top choices. Now how do you go about finding homes that are available in your target neighborhood without getting pressured by salespeople? There are several methods that you can use without leaving the comfort of your living room.

- *Realtor.com* – This website is a great resource which should be used constantly. You can find every piece of information regarding your target neighborhood in one place. However, I always recommend getting a variety of sources to feel safe that you are capturing what the market is really doing.

- *Real Estate Sections of Newspapers* – Although newspapers have taken a beating because most home sellers are listing online, there are still some really good deals that show up in the newspaper every day. Don't miss out on this opportunity just because it is the "old way" of doing things.

- *Owners.com* – These are the homes that are being sold by the owners themselves without the help of a real estate agent. They are referred to as "For Sale By Owner" (FSBO) and can yield some pretty good results for searches if used correctly.

- *Local websites of real estate agents* – These websites can give you neighborhood information, localized statistics and hot spots. They will usually be a little more specialized for a particular neighborhood than some of the bigger websites.

Finding What Comparable Homes Are Selling For In Your Target Neighborhood

During your research and travels I'm sure you will begin to see a pricing trend for houses you like. You will also notice that there are houses that you would not pay any amount to live in which are listed for a pretty penny. There is only one way to tell what is hot and what is not and that is by looking at the average range of houses that sold that are similar. The way for you to do that is by searching the following three websites:

- **www.visionappraisal.com** – This is the #1 online property sales online resource. You will find pictures, floor plans, previous sales amounts, as well as current homeowners. I could spend many more pages telling you about the benefits of this online resource, but let it suffice to say go their first and often when researching properties.

- *www.realestateabc.com* – Another great online resource which gives you up to thirty comparable properties when you enter an address and also provides additional supporting information for each property.

- ***www.zillow.com*** – This website has taken a bit of a beating in the last twenty four months, because the information sometimes comes back highly irregular with similar houses. Nonetheless, it is still a useful resource, which is pretty accurate eight out of ten times.

When you combine the information from these three sources what you have is a pretty good idea of the value, market temperature and amount of house you may be able to afford one.

Smart Home Buyer Program
Step #8

1. Find at least three neighborhoods which fit your criteria and do online research, drive-bys and meet the locals to learn:

   - Who the neighbors are
   - Crime rates
   - School system options
   - Hidden houses for sale

2. Write down the addresses of houses for sale. Go to www.visionappraisal.com and look up houses that were sold in the last six months. Make sure the houses are similar to the prospective house and within three miles of the house.

What is Coming Up Next ...

Now that you have done your homework and know several target neighborhoods, now it is time to hire a real estate agent. The next chapter tells you exactly how you can select a real estate agent you can trust to negotiate a fair price and terms.

CHAPTER 9

The Agent Advantage
The Best Ways to Select the Right Real Estate Agent to Help You Find & Negotiate Your Purchase

Purchasing a house is a daunting proposition. In case no one has clued you in yet, then let me be the first to tell you. The path to homeownership can be nerve wracking, frustrating, but also very rewarding when the final papers are signed.

Trying to even figure out whether or not to go with a real estate agent is probably the most daunting task of all next to getting approved for a mortgage. Why? It is because each real estate agent operates differently. Even though Mary Lou Smith down the street had great luck with Century 21, that does not mean you will also have good luck. Knowing what to look for in your real estate agent is the first thing every new home buyer should be aware of as they are starting to look for their perfect home.

In this chapter I'm going to discuss what to look for in your real estate agent, how to find the right house under your agent's guidance, and what to look for when working with a real estate agent to keep from being duped.

A Behind The Scenes Look At A Real Estate Agent

A real estate agent is someone who has gone through the many months of real estate school to obtain a state authorized license to help you buy (or sell) your home. They act as your agent to negotiate prices with the buyer or seller so that a transaction can be finalized allowing you to buy your new home.

A good real estate agent is worth their weight in gold and helps you:

- Hone in on your true needs and wants.
- Find a home you like which meets your goals.
- Get the background information on the property.
- Puts together an offer price to give to seller.
- Negotiate with the sellers.
- Your go-to person for the whole purchase transaction.
- Put together the purchase and sales contract.

However a bad real estate agent can cause you many days and nights of anguish by:

- Steering you towards a certain neighborhood you do not really like
- Locking you into a long term agreement and won't let you out
- Failing to disclosing vital information about the property
- Not researching and verifying the property presented in the listing
- Being in cahoots with the sellers or seller's agent.
- Simply not knowing enough to be your go-to person for your purchase.

You've Got To Be Kidding Me...Right?

From the very beginning Brian and Angela knew that finding a home they could afford would be darn near impossible. However, they didn't let their fear stand in the way. That's why when they bumped into Patricia at Stop & Shop, who was a real estate agent, they were thrilled. Patricia claimed to have the inside track on several soon-to-be on-the-market houses so they were all ears. Pat seemed very knowledgeable and was more than helpful. The only real issue Brian and Angela had with using her to represent them was that her availability was limited to only Wednesday and Friday evenings after 6:30 pm and every second and fourth weekend a month.

Brian was the first one to voice his concern over waiting for several days between going to see the best deals. And for the first couple of months Angela was the one to be supportive of Pat's limited schedule. It wasn't until they happened to drive by the perfect home for sale right in their target neighborhood on the morning drive to work, that they were upset. The same house was pending for sale by the afternoon on the way home from work. It was then that they finally realized why signing a six-month exclusive buyer's agreement with a part-time agent might have been a costly mistake.

Types of Real Estate Agents

There are three different levels of experience, knowledge and training when it comes to real estate agents. The differences are very important because you can reasonably expect a certain level of knowledge and expertise when working with each type of real estate agent.

Real Estate Agent – A professional who has completed several months of training and classroom education and been authorized by the state. This is the most basic level of real estate agents.

Realtors ® - These are real estate agents or brokers who are members of the National Association of Realtors ®. Their membership allows them to use a special designation, however they are held to a much higher standard than the average real estate agent. A Realtor ® will have more education and certifications as well. You will want to find an Accredited Buyer Representative (ABR) or Accredit Buyer Representative Manager (ABRM). This means they specialize in representing buyers. Your goal should always be to work with Realtor, because they usually have the highest level of experience and education.

Real Estate Brokers – Brokers have more education and knowledge than a basic real estate agent and manages an office or team of agents. Acts much more like a business owner in many regards.

Finding Your Own Buyer's Agent

Finding a good real estate agent who is knowledgeable, experienced and trustworthy should be your number one priority. However, you must be sure the real estate agent's expertise matches up as closely as possible with your dream home list requirements you created when you first started the home buying process. Once that is done, you must consider the following variables with every real estate agent you may be considering:

- **Location** – Don't hire a real estate agent who only works in a certain county and you live three counties over.

- **Style** – There are some real estate agents who only specialize in hotels and occasionally take on a buyer or two for residential property. You should avoid them at all costs unless you are looking for a hotel.

- **Construction** – Many home buyers would love to purchase newly constructed homes, but did you know that these homes have a whole different set of issues and unless a real estate agent specializes in these, he or she won't have a clue about what to do.

- **Size** – Sounds obvious, but over the years I have seen many people buy homes that were too big and too small from persuasive real estate agents...all because they loved how the house looked.

- **Age** – The newer the home, the more likely that it will have the bells and whistles you might like. The older the home, the more you might have to update once you move in. An experienced real estate agent will know this.

- **Functionality** – An experienced agent will ask you questions about your lifestyle to find those little "extras" that make you glad you bought your home.

- **Land** – Unbelievable as it might sound there are some of us who actually need a 96-acre lake to fish for bass every weekend. However, if that is your dream home and your real estate agent specializes in land-locked condos, you might be in for a bit of a disappointment.

Before making a decision on a real estate agent you should definitely reference your Dream Home Checklist. After you determine your needs and wants, the type of real estate agent you should be looking for becomes crystal clear. Otherwise you could find yourself with a real estate agent who really wants to help you, but does not have the expertise to truly help you find your ideal home.

Recommended Methods To Find A Real Estate Agent

The number one method for finding a quality real estate agent is to ask your friends, family and co-workers for a recommendation. Then you will want to go online to the National Association of Exclusive Buyers Agents, at www.naeba.org to cross-reference their name to see if they specialize as buyers' agents only. You will learn why that is so important a little later on, but for the next five minutes just trust me.

The second way to find an agent is to look online. This is an easy way to do it. You can instantly find out which agents are really moving and shaking when it comes to having houses for sale. However, keep in mind that these agents represent the sellers, so you will want to enter in search terms like "shoreline condo buyer's agent" to get more specific search results when looking online.

It is also worth your time to visit realtor.com or activerain.com. However, one of the most underrated strategies I have seen is to actually enter the search term "exclusive buyer brokerage, no listings" for whatever area you want to live in and you will find agents who specialize in working with buyers just like you.

The Worst Way To Find A Good Real Estate Agent

Attending open houses looking for an agent is like rolling the dice. The agent who is doing the open house may or may not be the listing agent, BUT they absolutely know the listing agent and thus is more likely to be torn between negotiating the best price for you and helping out their buddy. This is not guaranteed to happen, but in my experience, is just more likely to happen. However, with that being said, visiting opening houses is a good opportunity to find out about the house and what comparable houses are selling for.

How Your Real Estate Agent Gets Paid

Your real estate agent, whether they are representing you in purchasing the home or selling it, is paid via a commission or percentage of the final sales price of the home. Their pay comes directly from the sales proceeds and usually you never have to worry about how the commission is paid. This is done behind the scenes, so you probably won't know it's happening. If there are two agents involved – a listing agent and a buying agent – the money for the commission goes into an escrow fund and then is split between the two agents when the house is closed on and the transaction finalized. A single agent, representing both parties obviously keeps the entire commission to themselves.

This is a very simplified explanation. We will take a look at it in more detail with the following example. A home is selling for $300,000 with a six percent commission for the agents. Money has been placed in escrow for the transaction of the home. When the sale of the home closes and all of the papers are signed, the company holding the money in escrow will issue two commission checks from the escrow account totaling $18,000 or 6% of the selling price.

Each real estate agent's broker receives $9,000 and then the agent gets a certain percentage of that amount. What the agent receives goes for advertising expenses, errors and omissions insurance, gas from driving the clients to the houses, and other expenses that may have built up over the length of time it took to sell the house.

A Critical Look At Small Real Estate Offices

Utilizing the small town real estate agent may seem a great way to promote community spirit and solidarity, but be prepared to have to look for your home on a limited time schedule. More often than not, the small real estate firm closes at 5pm on the dot and some may not even work on the weekend. If the only day you can look at a house is on Sunday at 2:45pm, you better make sure the appointment is in place prior to 5pm Friday night.

Larger company real estate offices are open on the weekends and available to fit your schedule, not theirs. Also, small agencies may not have the newest equipment available to them and they are not always in the loop with the escrow and mortgage companies like larger firms are. Now, I'm not saying that all small "Mom and Pop" real estate agencies are this way, especially since more businesses and homes have computers and the Internet to help keep them up to date. I'm just saying that you should be aware that sometimes the smaller real estate offices fall behind the times.

Interviewing Your Real Estate Agent

At the end of the day, no matter how you select an agent, there is a standard template set of questions and pearls of wisdom that apply.

- **Are you a full-time agent or do you have another job? How many buyers have you helped purchase new homes this year?**

  An active agent is more likely to be up-to-date on the market and the law.

- **How many buyers have you helped purchase homes in the neighborhood I'm looking to buy in?**

  You want a real estate agent with local expertise, so a few sales in the neighborhood is a good thing.

- **What are some of the things that have gone wrong and reasons clients in the past have been unhappy with your services?**

  Knowing why others had issues will give you some insight into potential problems for you later on down the line.

- **Have you ever had a client file a complaint with your broker or the state against you?**

  Do not get squeamish about asking this one. You can also check with the state licensing division for real estate agents.

- **How much do you charge for your fee?**

  Although the seller normally pays the buyer's agent, there could be times where you have to come to closing with the money to pay your agent.

- **Do you offer additional services other than negotiating my real estate transactions?**

What you really are trying to get at is what other fees you will be paying for by working with them.

- **At what point am I considered to be working with you?**

Most buyers do not realize that having an agent drive you around to look at homes could legally obligate you to work with that agent even without a contract.

- **How many short sales or foreclosures have you sold in the last year?**

These types of properties can be big profits, but they require a ton of long paperwork. The agent must have experience with doing these or you can face some legal liability.

- **Do you have a team that will also be working with us?**

Most agents have a team of assistants and helpers. However, if you are paying the agent then the agent is the one you should be dealing with primarily.

- **Are you going to show me every property for sale that meets my criteria?**

Sounds obvious, but some agents definitely steer buyers because for-sale-by-owner properties do not pay a commission.

- **What is the soonest you can get me in to see a home after I call you?**

The best homes are snatched up fast so your agent has to be quick on their feet.

- **Do you or have you ever represented the seller and buyer on the same house?**

It is not possible for a real estate agent to fairly and properly represent both the buyer and seller...no matter what they tell you.

- **What is your specialty?**

  You want an expert and not just someone who is happy to get a client.

- **How do we handle the situation if I'm unhappy and want to end our contract?**

  A good agent has a guarantee that addresses your concerns when this happens.

Do You Really Have To Hire A Real Estate Agent?

If you are a first-time home buyer, then yes you should hire a real estate agent to represent you. So, that means that there will be at least two agents involved in the transaction. One agent represents you, the buyer. The other agent – whose name you typically see on the 'For Sale' signs in front of the houses that is on the market – represents the seller.
The seller wants to get as much money out of their house as possible, while you want to buy for the best or lowest deal available. The two real estate agents will work together as legal representative of you and the seller to come to an agreed upon price that is usually somewhere in between the highest amount of money you will pay for the house and the lowest amount of money the seller will accept.

ALWAYS, ALWAYS, ALWAYS use a different real estate agent than the one selling the house. The agent representing the seller is going to try to get the most money out of you to give to the seller if you both use the same person. Trying to find a real estate agent who can be neutral and represents you both equally is like searching for a needle in a haystack, not impossible, just very unlikely. In case you didn't hear me the first time, you should NEVER use the same real estate agent as the home seller.

The Infamous Part-time Real Estate Agent

Obviously, part time agents work part time. However, let me

explain how that affects you. See, part-time agents tend to have another 9-5 job that is their main paying job. Therefore, selling real estate is a side job. Yes, all part-time agents have to go through some form of training and be licensed in order to buy and sell real estate, but the fact that they cannot devote their time to you and their other clients except on a limited basis is really not going to help you get the undivided attention and personal guidance you will need.

It is also very difficult to schedule showings with a part time agent. Your time could be limited to going to see properties in the evenings or on the weekends only, and depending on your own schedule, the weekends may not be convenient for you.

Unfortunately, more often than not, by using a part-time agent you are not getting the right professional service you are entitled to receive. Additionally, many part time real estate agents have not built up a relationship with other agents in the area to the point where they do favors for one another, like letting it slip that a certain house is getting set to go on the market or forgoing a commission to help the clients out. They may not be aware of changes in real estate law that could affect the home sale. These are all factors that should be remembered when you are tempted to let your newly licensed cousin help you buy or sell your home.

Of course, if the agent is part-time because they are partially retired from the real estate business in the first place, that is a whole different story.

Tips For Signing An Exclusive Agreement With One Agent

An exclusive agent buyer's agreement is a form that states that you will only work with one specific real estate agent. This form guarantees you that your real estate agent is working for you. This may seem obvious, until you realize that many agents will do the minimal amount of work to find your ideal home, unless they have an agreement signed. However, I have heard of horror stories where an agent emails over a buyer's broker agreement before even meeting with buyers. Once you find the agent that meets the interview guidelines, then you should absolutely expect to sign a buyer's broker agreement before having that good agent roll out the red carpet, limo, and champagne. After all, the buyer's broker agreement is to protect both you and the agent.

The biggest reason that most buyers are hesitant about signing the buyer's agreement is because they do not want to be locked into a deal with the agent from hell. So here is what you do to protect yourself:

- **Get a Short-Term Agreement** - There is no standard time for an agreement. You can simply ask for a 60-day or 90-day agreement at most. I have even heard of a 24-hour and seven day agreement.

- **Ask for a Non-Exclusive Agreement** - By using this agreement you agree to pay the agent if you switch during the process on a home that agent showed you. The agent is protected and you can use any other agent you wish.

- **Meet-In-The-Middle** - Let the agent know you need more time before signing an agreement. Use the try before you buy statement. It is only fair to see how the agent works before you agree to put the largest financial decision of your life into their hands.

- **Clearly State The Terms and Areas** - You can simply let the agent know that you want his or her services for a certain neighborhood and price range. If you go outside of that area and price range then you are not legally obligated to compensate them.

- **Get a Guarantee** - A good agent will give his buyers a guarantee. This means that you can end the buyer's agreement at any time if you are not satisfied and your agent can leave at any time if they are not satisfied.

Searching For A Home When Your Real Estate Agent Is Not Available

There are three main ways to do this, but only one that I suggest you use in order to discover the real bargains:

- Drive around neighborhoods looking at houses
- Look in the newspapers, real estate weekly publications or online
- Give your real estate agent your own requirements. Such as target neighborhood, price range etc.

Driving around the neighborhood you are interested in moving into and seeing what is on the market seems to be one of the easiest ways to find a home. You drive around and if there should happen to be an open house going on, stop and tour the home. Otherwise, you can just write down the addresses of the homes on the market and the real estate agent that has the home listing for you to research on the Internet.

This particular method of looking for a home is great for new home buyers who really have no idea what type of home they are looking for. Unfortunately, this method also limits you on what you can see. Does the home have a backyard? Does it have it swimming pool? What about the number of bedrooms? How much is being asked for it? These are all things that, as a new home buyer, you need to decide upon before looking for a new house. Driving around and logging homes for research is fine if you are doing it as part of another trip away from your current home. It is not an efficient way to find the house you actually want to place an offer on.

With the Internet being prevalent in most homes, searching for houses online is a very simple and easy to use method. You also get considerably more information about the homes on the market – and the ones you have logged during your drives – than you do when just driving around the neighborhood. You will be able to eliminate homes on your list as you research them for not having the amenities you are looking for, being out of your price range, or simply just not being what you really want. Online listings can tell you how many bedrooms are in the home, the sizes of all the rooms, how it is heated or cooled, the size of the yard, the school district the home is in, and more. Many of these real estate websites also have photos of the inside of the home or even 'virtual tours', small movie clips that show you the entire home.

Real Estate Agent's Have Feelings Too!

Be careful of allowing multiple real estate agents to show you properties, because it could cause a disaster later on. Yes...even if you have not signed an agreement.

There have been many times when real estate agents have tied up properties and commissions, because of an overzealous buyer. It's usually because buyers don't realize that any time a real estate agent shows you a house that you later end up buying, they have essentially performed the duties of an unwritten contract.

Of course you should consult your legal counsel on your specific situation if you find yourself in this predicament.

Going To Multiple Open Houses

When you have a full time real estate agent working for you, they will be looking for the type of house that meets your requirement for you and they will provide you with up to date listings from the local MLS based on your requirements. Curious buyers who think a house may look nice on the outside and want to see the inside go to open houses. Plus, open houses do not allow you to screen for your criteria before parking your vehicle, getting out, and going inside to find out the hard way.

Real estate agents are valuable because they screen your requirements against all of the listings available so that you do not waste time. Open houses for people with real estate agents are good for one thing only: decorating ideas for your own home. If you decide you want to see the inside of a house, then go to an open house, but be sure to let the agent working at the site know that you are already under contract with another agent and that you are there simply to get some ideas. They will then focus their concentration on potential customers and let you wander around at your leisure.

Three Sneaky Little Tricks To Avoid With Real Estate Agents

While we would prefer to think of everyone as being honest, some real estate agents can pull the wool over the eyes of their clients to the point where the clients have been righteously ripped off – both buyer and seller. There are some tricks in their arsenal that will cause a buyer to sometimes commit to a home that they know is way over their price range and simply out of reach. Here we are going to discuss some of these real estate agent tricks so that you as a new home buyer, are aware that your agent could be trying to con you.

- **"We just got three offers on the house. You need to move fast on it."**

    If a house has been on the market for quite a long time, the real estate agent may be feeling pressure to get it sold from their boss or the seller themselves. In order to get what they feel is the best client to 'move' to a decision on the house, they will call and tell the buyer that someone else has made and offer on the house. This is a ploy to get the buyer stirred up and possible offer more on the house than what they originally wanted to spend. With the offer in hand, the buyer cannot change easily and the sale could go through for more than what the buyer really wanted to commit to.

More often than not, there are no other offers on the home. If the seller even catches wind that they will not be able to sell the house for the price they want, they will push their agent to do whatever it takes to get the price they want. Beware of additional offers that suddenly appear out of thin air from your agent or the seller's agent. If you think there is something fishy about the other offers, decline putting in one of your own and move to your second choice house. The last thing you want to do is commit to a house that will be more than you can afford and not pleasing all around.

- **The showing order switcheroo**

   Some real estate agents believe that the order they show the house to the potential buyer will make an impact on their final decision. For example, if a buyer wishes to look at five different houses they like, the real estate agent can make a list of the homes, and decide how they are going to view them, leaving the 'best' house for last. It is the goal of the agent that when they get back to the office, the client will have that 'best' house in their heads and that will be the one they make the offer on. In reality that 'best' house in the five could actually be the worst.

   Some agents will also do some serious trash talking about a bunch of houses the potential buyer wants to see if they are all of a comparable value and quality. What the agent will do in this situation is show you the most expensive and best house in the bunch that you want to look at first. Then at each of the next four houses the agent shows you, they will tell and point out every problem the house has and all of the negative aspects of the house in order to veer you away and back to the first house – the one they really want you to buy – in order to get you to place an offer.

   If you have a strict budget and the real estate agent seems to be playing one of these tricks on you, stick to your guns and do not let the agent swing you away from the house you are interested in. You are the one that is going to have to live there and many of the things the agent may claim to be as 'negative' aspects of the house are probably just things that a good coat of paint and new carpet will take care of.

- **The seller gets to choose all of the services**

  This is not always the case because of the way the economy and interest rates fluctuate. A seller's market is when they can set a higher price to sell for, interest rates are up, and people are buying homes at a comfortable rate. A buyer's market is when interest rates are low and buyers can haggle sellers into a lower price bracket in order to sell. It is usually the buyer's end of the transaction that deals with the escrow company, not the seller. The buyer goes to the escrow company and signs the documents. The seller does not.

  When buying a house you always need to discuss this with your real estate agent and see what their procedures on the matter are. There is absolutely no reason why the buyer cannot have a say in the escrow company that is going to be used. Your real estate agent can argue and work this out for you so that you are not traveling out of your way because the seller chose a company five minutes from him and seventy miles away from you.

  Real estate agents build up friendships and working relationships with other real estate professionals in the buying and selling business. They usually only work with people they trust in the business. Sometimes, though, it is not convenient for the client and so real estate agents on both sides of the fence should be willing to work with the seller on what escrow company is going to be the best for them to use. The same goes for the title insurance, but in most cases, the title insurance is the responsibility of the seller.

Smart Home Buyer Program
Step #9

1. Review your Dream Home Checklist and ask your friends, family and co-workers for a recommendation of Realtors they've worked with. If you do not get a recommendation then follow the next step to find one.

2. Go online to the National Association of Exclusive Buyers Agents at www.naeb.com to see if your real estate agent is listed. If you cannot find them at that website go online to their own personal website to learn if they are exclusive buyer's agents.

3. Interview the real estate agent by phone or meet in person to get all of the questions answered. Follow the tips for signing an exclusive contract with one agent.

What is Coming Up Next ...

Now that you have hired a real estate agent. The next chapter gives you details on how find hidden bargains.

CHAPTER 10

Do Your Homework Before You Buy
Quick and Easy Ways to Perform Due Diligence on a Potential Property that You Plan to Purchase

Peeling back the layers of information in order to get at the truth about a house is a very important skill which you must become proficient at doing.

The reason why is simply this; if you sign a purchase and sales agreement, then slap down your hard earned money, only to find out the house is a complete and utter disaster next door to the worst serial sex offender in the history of the state, it does not matter how good of a deal you just got because you are up a creek with a paddle the size of a plastic spoon.

When you are doing your research or walking through the property you should be asking your real estate agent questions, but DO NOT ever let the sellers or their real estate agent see your excitement or emotion. If you do, you risk losing control and overpaying because the only time you should let your emotion shine through is if you are pointing out an issue that you spot. When you do see something you make sure you say it loud enough so that both real estate agents hear as well as the home seller.

Now here is an overview of the seven steps to get the insider truth on any property you are thing about buying.

> **Step #1** – Search sex offender registry
> **Step #2** – Ask for the seller's disclosure form
> **Step #3** – Visit the property at least four different times
> **Step #4** – Drive around your target neighborhood

Step #5 – Research at the local government offices
Step #6 – Inspecting the inside of the house
Step #7 – Inspecting the outside of the house

These steps have been compiled after many years of watching home buyers make mistake after mistake. Follow these steps and you can rest assured that you will know just as much about the house and neighborhood as the current owners know.

Step #1: Search The State And National Registry For Known Sex Offenders Living In The Prospective Neighborhood

This has to be the most often overlooked first step that first-time home buyers forget to do. And do not even think about telling me you do not have children because everyone has…

Nieces
Nephews
Visiting friends or family with children
A spouse or significant other

The real question you should be asking is, "When will your loved one come by for a visit?" Without a doubt this is the most important first step you should take when considering a home.

Once you have the information the choice is then yours to decide whether or not you want to proceed forward with living in a neighborhood with one or many known sex offenders. To complete a search for sex offenders go to www.google.com and enter "sex offender's database" and you will have several links to online databases.

Step #2: Ask for seller's disclosure statement

The second thing you should do is ask for the seller's disclosure statement from your real estate agent or the sellers themselves. The seller's disclosure is a form that is required by law, which lets you know the following:

- **Title** – reveals any issues or disputes against the ownership of the sellers. It is also a written and legal document with the seller's claiming to be the true owners and thus have the legal right to sell the property.

- **Structure** – covers all code violations for any reason on the entire property.

- **Land** – reveals if the home sits on a fault line, flood zone or unstable earth foundation.

- **Environment** – has there been any problems with nearby businesses, construction or homes that would pose an environmental threat.

- **Homeowner's Association** – reveals if the owner has additional monthly payments for any other type of service that is provided in relation to the home.

- **Plumbing** – discloses the condition, location and general condition of the system

- **Appliances** – covers if there have been issues with the gas, electricity and functionality of any appliances included in the sale.

- **Heating and air conditioning systems** – gives you an insight into what can cause major issues in one of the major home systems.

- **Other & Additional** – discloses everything else like pest problems, damaged roof or incomplete construction etc.

Beware Seller's Disclosure

While getting a seller's disclosure as early in the process as possible is usually advisable, you should take it with a grain of salt. Most rookie buyers stop researching as soon as they receive the seller's disclosure. This is a HUGE mistake. You should use the seller's disclosure as a guide, but never as the final authority.

Step #3: Visit the property AT LEAST four times

There is no way you should even consider buying a home until you have looked at it several times at different hours of day and night. You will not be able to get good feeling for the area without doing this step.

You will want to see the home at the worst hours because you will most likely be living there twenty-four seven, three hundred sixty five days a year. The next visit after the initial visit should be a weeknight and you should be looking for proper street lighting, flow of traffic, suspicious looking characters.

Then you should visit it during the day and night on a weekend because that is when you will have a chance to really hit the goldmine of information by meeting the neighbors.

Step #4: Walk & Drive Through The Surrounding Neighborhood

One of the greatest sources of information you will ever come across in your search is the neighbors of the particular house you are interested in. The neighbors will know how often the previous homeowners upgraded the exterior of the home, how they maintained the yard and their overall pride of ownership.

The best way to "bump" into the neighbors is to go for a nice evening walk in the neighborhood to see if anyone is outside doing yard work or playing with the kids. If you find someone, simply spark up a conversation stating that you are thinking about moving into the neighborhood and what is their experience been like.

During the conversation be sure to get specific about the

house you are interested in. For example, some good questions to ask are:

- How long did or have the owners lived there?

- If you could do it over again would you choose the same neighborhood again?

- Have there been any major renovations on the house recently?

- How did they take care of the house over the years?

- Have there been any crimes committed in the house?

- Are there things that happen at certain times of year that are noticeable?

I would even suggest asking the neighbors about the previous owners prior to the current owners. If they have the contact information then you should ask for it. No one will know as much about the house as someone who has lived in it over an extended period of time. The point is to ask as many questions as possible, because that is the only way to get as many answers as you need to make an intelligent decision.

The neighbors will also be able to give you a good feel of the general attitude of the community. Are they friendly or standoffish? Is the neighborhood mostly comprised of renters or older people? Is there an informal or formal neighborhood association? Those types of questions and observations reveal tons of information about the neighborhood.

Waiting behind a school bus while it is dropping off kids in the morning might not seem like a big deal when you first go to visit the property, but it will be a completely different story when you are stuck behind a school bus for an extra fifteen minutes every morning when you are leaving for work. In order to really observe the traffic patterns, you must go first visit the property in the morning when schools are starting and in the afternoon when schools are letting out and parents are coming home from work.

That is the best way to get the inside scoop on traffic patterns. Do not minimize this step because it seems trivial. By the way, when you are walking the neighborhood you should also be looking for school crossing signs, school bus stops, traffic lights and stop signs. It is also a good idea to call up the police station and ask them if there have been a lot of issues with speeding in the neighborhood.

When you are walking around the neighborhood you should also be watching out for any type of contractors sign on homes or in the yards. Jot down the number, because you will definitely want to call up these folks and ask them about the home, area or general take on the neighborhood.

Imagine knowing in advance that several people on the same side of the street have hired someone to repair their home's foundation in the last several months. That could possibly mean there is some type of earth movement beneath the street. Or you could even possible find out who did home repairs on the home you are thinking about buying. That would be a huge bonus, but you will never know if you do not take the time to write down the numbers and call them up.

Just like with the neighbors, if you let them know you are considering purchasing in the area and need some background information; they will be just as inquisitive about you as a potential neighbor as you are about the prospective home.

Step 5

Researching At The Local Government Level

During the course of your house investigation you will need to purchase manila folders to contain all of the various copies and research you turn up on the property. It should be your number one goal to get copies of every piece of information the city department would allow you to. This is important because your detective work will require you to visit several if not all of the following places and it is very unlikely that you will remember all of this stuff in your head.

The major offices you should visit in person or online are:

- Tax Assessors Office (Tax Collector and City or Town Clerk)
- Building Department (also known as Code Enforcement)
- Planning & Zoning Department
- Public Works Department

Tax Assessors Office

The tax assessor's office is the first place you should visit, because it will give you an idea of how the city actually views the property you are considering. This is very important because the tax assessor will determine how the property is valued and consequently taxed.

FYI, there have been many times when I have seen the assessors information vary dramatically from the information that is being shared on the listing of the home.

When visiting the tax assessor's office you are looking for the following information:

Current and previous ownership history
- Ownership deed
- Sale prices
- Sale dates
- Land area
- Lot frontage
- Zoning class
- Available utilities
- Assessor's tax map

Building construction details
- Heating
- Electrical
- Plumbing
- Date of construction
- Permit numbers
  - Dates of remodeling
  - Renovations performed
  - Building size
  - Sketches with measurements
- Room counts
- Other building features / amenities
- References to other site / subdivision plans
- Any other additional notes and comments
- Tax Rate (or Mill Rate)

While gathering this information you will want to keep your eyes out for information that will give you insight into:

- Real estate tax history for the property
- Overall real estate tax trends
- Most recent full assessment
- How they calculate assessed value
- Are there any citywide contracts negotiations underway which could impact real estate taxes such as Police, Fire or Teacher Union contracts?

You will also want to know what major highway or road and public utilities projects are on the horizon that could possibly impact real estate taxes.

Not knowing about major construction projects can result in you being completely side-blinded when your taxes increase by over 50% like they recently did in a town near me. There were homeowners who taxes went from $3,200 per year to over $4,800 a year. Talk about lifestyle adjustment!

Building Department

This is where you will find out things such as have they made any legal changes to the property. When walking in be sure to let them know that you are contemplating buying a certain property and want to do your homework. By the way, it is possible for them not to have information on a property because nothing has been done. And then there are other times when you will need a trash bag to hold all of the paperwork. It just depends.

The Building Department for a home could contain:

- Previous requests for renovation permits
- The actual permit approvals or denials
- Lot line disputes or changes
- Future construction plans
- Floor plans
- Previous inspections
- Violations
- Requests or denials for zoning variances

It is also a good idea to get the contact information for the contractor's names on the permits because they will be a good source of information for potential issues.

Planning & Zoning Department

One of the most worrisome and troubling times as a homeowner is when your neighborhood is being rezoned to allow for business and developments. Trust me when I tell you that construction projects can dramatically alter your lifestyle. By the way, usually there is nothing you can do to stop this from happening.

Every town, city, community and village goes through this type of transition. My goal is to provide you with the tools to see it coming and not be taken by surprise. The way to find out this information is by actually going over the master plan that the city has for your neighborhood. Each city has one of those big life-size maps in their planning and zoning office, which clearly outlines the next five to ten years worth of developments for everyone to see. You will want to look to see what subdivisions, businesses or general construction projects are slated for your area.

The planning and zoning ordinances will clearly spell out each owner's lot, yard size and type of property that can be built in certain areas. Zoning changes can have such a huge impact on your life so you will want to know the following:

- Is the house you are considering zoned for residential use?
- Is a different zoning area next to the property?
- Is the property in two different zones?
- What are the minimum lot requirements?

You will also want to make sure that you know if your property is legally non-conforming or grandfathered in. Legal non-conforming means that the house was constructed before the current zoning plans were in place.

Registry of Deeds/Courthouse

The courthouse or registry of deeds is where you will find the technical and exact legal description of the property. It will detail the following:

- Legal right-of-ways to neighboring properties
- Streets that may appear on maps but do not actually exist
- Legal rights to common areas around the property
- Neighborhood sanitary systems
- Any type of land exceptions for preservation and conservation

Pumping Utility Companies For Information

This next little tip I am about to share with you is one that 99.9% of home buyers have never even thought of. It involves actually calling the utility companies with the home address of the property you are investigating and asking for annual cost or average monthly usage. If the usage is high then it can indicate that there is a problem in the area with electrical lines, inefficient insulation, water pressure problems etc.

Step #6: Inspecting The Outside Of The House

Now it is time to look at the exterior of the house and see how it measures up to your taste and research information. It is very important that in this phase you guard your expressions, feeling and thoughts until you are out of the presence of the seller's and their agent.

The major things that you are looking for are:

Foundation
- Do you notice any cracks?
- Are there any repaired cracks?

Roof
- Do you observe any tree sap or mold on the roof?
- Is there any sagging anywhere?
- Where are the vents or chimney?
- Do you see any lifted or curled shingles?
- Are there multiple layers of shingles?

Siding
- What is the material made of?
- Does it look old and worn out?
- Can you actually get a paint chip or color type?
- Does the wood look like it is peeling or splintering apart?
- Do you see the right type of caulking?
- Do you observe mold?

Trim (shadow boards, and overhangs)
- Is the trim complete or is some absent?
- Is the paint peeling?
- Do you see broken, rotted or cracked trim?

Windows
- Are there any missing, cracked or broken?
- What type of material are the windows made of?
- Are the windows insulated?
- Do you see storm windows?

Doors
- What type of material are the doors made of?
- Are they stained or painted?

Every house will have different construction and materials, but what you are looking for is to see the general condition and to make sure that you have every piece of information that you need to make an informed decision.

Step #7: Inspecting the Inside Of The House

By inspecting the inside of the house, you will be able to point out any difference between what the seller's or bank is telling you and what the city says they have.

If you do not know where to begin here are some questions to open up the conversation (Yes, you may already know the answers, but you are just trying to get the ball rolling) here are some sample questions to ask the sellers:

- When did you buy the property?
- When did you put the house on the market?
- Have you already selected another place to live? If so, when do you have to be there?
- When are you planning on moving?
- What type of work have you done to the house since buying it?
- Did you do the work yourself or contract it out?
- Do you have the contractors contact information?

- Was the contractor's work guaranteed for a period of time? If so, how long?
- Did you get the permits from the town to do the work?
- Have you ever been required to file an insurance claim due to damage?
  - If so what was it and who repaired it?

The following are places you should look within the house:

Floors

- How old are the floorboards?
- Gaps between boards
- Split boards
- Cracked tiles
- Cracked and missing grout between tiles or along wall and baseboards
- Are there any diagonal cracks above doors and windows?
- Do floors sag?
- Do floors have spring in them?
- Do floors squeak or creak?

Bathrooms

- Check around the toilet and tub/shower for soft or spongy flooring.
- Flush the toilet to check pressure.
- Lift the tank cover and check to see if the flush valve is new or old.
- Watch for leaks around base of bowl.
- Check water connections for age and corrosion
- Run water in tubs and sinks to check for possible blocked drains
- Faucets, check water pressure and for uneven water stream
- Is there any dripping after you shut off the water?

- Check all water connections for age and corrosion
- Is there a strong, vortex flow down the drain or does the water seem to drain slowly?
- Do the owners know if their water is hard or soft? Water described as "hard" is high in dissolved minerals, specifically calcium and magnesium.

Heating, Cooling and Electrical Systems

It is very important that you know and recognize that the major systems in the house are very expensive to replace and repair, so you need to get the contact information of any contractor, company or service man that has done work on the house.

- Test all the light switches
- Are the lights flickering which indicate the fuses may have too many circuits
- Do you see any ceiling fans?
- Do you hear any humming noises when you turn switches on?
- What type of heating system does the house use?
- How often have the sellers changed the filters?
- What type of fuel does the heating system use?
- If oil or propane is used, where are the fuel storage tanks?
- If electric heat, is it baseboard or radiant?
- What is the age of the heating system?
- Is there any central cooling system?
- What size is it?
- Does it adequately cool the entire home?
- How old is it?

Kitchen Appliances

- Do all the appliances work without any problems whatsoever?
- How old are the appliances?

- Have they ever required servicing?

Doors, Windows, and Cabinets

- Do all doors and windows open to the extent you would expect?
- Do any stick?
- Do any not open all the way?
- Do any stay closed?
- Do all of the locks and latches function, as they should?
- Is there any cabinet hardware missing?
- Do all kitchen drawers slide in an out smoothly?
- Are there any that have broken drawer slides?
- Are there any doors missing doorstops, which would allow the doorknob to smash into the wall when opened?

General Storage

- Does each bedroom have a closet?
- Is there a linen closet?
- Is there a pantry?
- Is there a utility closet?
- Do the closets have ample depth?
- Do the closets have ample shelving?

Basement

- Are there shut-offs for all the water lines/supplies?
- If you end up buying the house, BE SURE to have the seller show you where all the shut-offs are.
- Is any part of the basement finished?
- Does the basement feel damp?
- Does the basement look damp?
- If you can see any sections of the foundation, do you see any cracks?

Attic

- Ask if there is an attic and how it is accessed.

- Check for any signs of dampness, rodent infestation or overall shabby conditions.

Smart Home Buyer Program
Step #10

1. Select a target home you want to focus on. Meet with your real estate agent and write down notes about everything you learn about the property.

2. Follow the seven steps to get the insider truth on any property you are thing about buying.

   Step #1 – Search sex offender registry
   Step #2 – Ask for seller's disclosure form
   Step #3 – Visit the property at least four different times
   Step #4 – Drive and walk around target neighborhood
   Step #5 – Research at the local government offices
   Step #6 – Inspecting the inside of the house
   Step #7 – Inspecting the outside of the house

   What is Coming Up Next ...

The next chapter shows you how to protect yourself from getting ripped off and losing the shirt off your back when buying your first home.

Smart Home Buyer Program
Step #11

1. Select three local real estate law firms to contact and ask to represent you during your home purchase.
2. Interview the attorney using the real estate attorney questionnaire worksheet.
3. Make your selection and bring your notebook with all of the information from your prospective homes for the attorney to review.

What is Coming Up Next ...

The next chapter reveals how you can negotiate the best deal on your home to get the best deal possible without feeling like you are taking advantage of the home seller's.

CHAPTER 11

How To Create An Irresistible Offer
Have Home Sellers Lining Up And Begging You To Buy Their Homes At Deep, Deep Discounts!

So you found a home that you want to buy and you think you are ready to go, but before you put in an offer you need to know how to even come up with an offer. This is an important lesson to learn early on in your home searching journey. If you offer too high, you can overpay and feel like you were tricked. However, if you bid too low you risk offending the seller and watching helplessly while your dream home slips through your fingers. When sitting down with your real estate agent and attorney, there are five different factors that should guide your offer amount.

- **Market Temperature** - When there are more houses than buyers then it is usually a good time to snatch up a deal. However, if you are buying in a more desirable neighborhood you may think you are in a buyer's market, but you are really in an isolated pocket which leans towards the seller getting close to asking price. Simply speaking, a buyer's market is a good time to bid low, while a seller's market requires offers to be closer to asking price.

- **Recently Sold Comparable Properties** - It is important to remember your offer should always be lower or comparable to what your neighbors paid for their house. The reason why this is true is because your mortgage lender will be doing the exact same thing in comparing your appraisal value to the neighbors. You may want to overbid to ensure you win the house, but it won't amount to a hill of beans if you can't get approved for a mortgage for that house.

- **Your Agents Advice** - If you followed my steps in the earlier chapter when selecting an agent, then you need to thoughtfully consider the guidance you receive from him or her. Your real estate agent will be able to let you know if your offer is reasonable and thus more likely to be accepted.

- **Seller's Goals** - Sometimes sellers want to quickly get rid of a home or are just testing the waters to see what their house might sell for. In either case your offer strategy would be different so you need to learn as much as possible about the sellers as you can.

- **Your Own Goals And Mindset** - Throughout the looking phase you are going to see homes being put under contract days after being on the market and you will also see homes languish on the market for many months. Your number one goal when thinking about an offer price is to NOT become emotional and make a quick, tired or confused decision about a home. Your decision should be ninety percent based on the numbers and facts and ten percent based on your emotion and heart.

Preparing Your Offer

Now, I must warn you that I'm about to say something that will be met by much resistance by many real estate agents, but it is my professional opinion based on both my client's experience and my own experience. Here it is; you should sit down with your real estate agent to go over your potential offer price but you should have your own real estate attorney prepare your offer to purchase or purchase and sales contract. That is right, I said it. You should hire an experienced real estate attorney to prepare your legally binding contract to buy a house.

The main reason is because when things go south as they sometimes do, you will have to hire an attorney, so why not have your attorney involved from day one. I feel so strongly about this that I devoted an entire chapter to this topic so feel free to skip ahead if you need convincing. Anyone who has ever lost a five thousand dollar deposit to a greedy home seller will agree that the cost of paying a couple hundred dollars for contract review more than pays for itself when you get your five thousand dollar deposit returned to them.

Now with that being said I do realize that each and every day there are many purchase transaction that go off without a hitch, however there is this magical force at play in the world called Murphy's Law. In case you are unfamiliar with Murphy's Law, let me give it to you in a nutshell. Murphy's Law simply states that what can go wrong *will* go wrong. It is that force that makes happy people suddenly think there is a world-wide conspiracy to ruin their home buying experience. I don't know about you, but it sure feels good to say "my attorney will be contacting you to discuss that" when you feel you are being treated unfairly.

Hints That You May Be Negotiating With A Flexible Seller

Here is when you know you may be able to work your negotiating mojo on the seller:

- The seller has already moved out before closing.
- Previous buyers backed out of purchasing.
- The price has been dropped several times.
- The house has sat on the market for a long time without being under contract.
- The listing says the seller is "motivated."
- The seller already has a must-move date in mind.
- There have been different agents representing the seller.
- The seller cannot move until this house is sold.

- The house is empty because the seller inherited the property but lives elsewhere
- The seller bought the house as an investment property but has little rental income coming in.

Offer To Purchase OR Purchase And Sales Contract

There are two options when it comes to writing up and ultimately presenting your offer to the sellers. I will review both and then give you some advice on my preferred method.

- **Offer To Purchase (also known as a Binder)** – Use this when you want to communicate that you have some level of interest in buying a certain property. Also use this to get the seller's to give you a tentative agreement in writing. This is not always viewed as legally binding because it is just an offer to purchase. The form will clearly spell out that it is not a legally binding purchase and sales contract so read carefully when using this form.

- **Purchase And Sales Contract** – Use this form when you are presenting an offer and deposit which you want to be legally binding once the seller signs it. The advantage is that it is legally binding once signed. The disadvantage of this form is that you must take a little extra time with your attorney or real estate agent to include your contingencies and word the language correctly to protect yourself.

The Purchase And Sales Contract

Be prepared to receive a purchase contract that is quite a few pages long and includes all of the information about your offer to buy the house. This form will be part of the final closing papers and will eventually go to the escrow and closing real estate attorney when the transaction is complete.

Once your offer is accepted, you as the buyer may be required to place what is called a good faith deposit on the house. This money will be held in escrow by the listing agent. The good faith deposit is a small percentage of the purchasing price, which will be applied towards your mortgage loan if the sale goes through. The deposit does not have to be very large, just large enough to make the seller feel comfortable about your intent and know that you are serious. Your real estate agent can advise on the best amount required.

The Language Of A Purchase And Sales Contract

It is very important that you know exactly what you are agreeing to do when you are completing your purchase and sales contract. If you are following the steps outlined in my book then there is simply no reason why you should be blind-sided by anything that is written in your contract. Here are some of the basic terms and definitions.

- **Parties** - You and the sellers name and contact information

- **A legal description of property** – Explains exactly what you are buying and how the city officially views the property

- **Offer or purchase price of property** – How much you agree to pay for the property

- **The date of the contract** – The date you signed the contract

- **The closing date** - The date you and the seller are expected to transfer payment and ownership to each other.

- **Down payment amount** – The amount you will contribute towards the purchase price in the form of cash or down payment assistance.

- **The terms of any escrow agreement** – The exact actions and or professional services used in order to hold the deposit money and perform certain services.

- **Contingencies** – Conditions to be met before transferring money and ownership

- **Title Condition** – The agreement that the seller will be able to sell a clear and trouble-free title of ownership to you.

- **Loan amount and conditions** – How much you are borrowing from a lender and the terms of your mortgage.

- **Resolving disputes** – How you and the seller will handle any issue that arises and cannot be resolved peaceably.

- **Personal property and fixtures** – What is included with the house when you buy it.

- **Usage rights** – What exactly you own and can use when you buy the property – more of a issue when buying condos, townhomes and co-ops.

- **Payment to agent** – The amount the real estate agents are getting compensated.

- **Additional Fees** – Covers various fees such as title insurance, deed preparation fees, notary fees, transfer taxes, escrow fees, title search fees etc.

- **Escrow holder** – The party holding the deposit funds.

- **Assessments and Proration's** – Details how the yearly taxes the sellers may have already paid, mortgage interest etc. will be paid and by whom

- **Contract expiration date** – When the contract expires and is no longer legally binding.

- **Damage to property** – Details what will happen if the house is damaged or destroyed while in escrow or under contract with you before closing.

- **Possession** – When the seller will move out and you can move in.

- **Time is of the essence** – You and the seller must have the closing before the expiration date or the contract is null and voided.

- **Seller representations** – Details the promise the seller states to be true about the condition of the house you are buying.

- **Entire agreement** – Statement insuring that the purchase and sales contract is the only agreement between you and the seller.

- **Signatures** – The final action that makes the contract legally binding.

The Most Popular Contingencies

Next to having an experienced real estate attorney write up the purchase and sales contract, there is no better leverage for protecting yourself than through contingencies. Using contingencies gives you the peace of mind of knowing you can legally back out of the transaction if some crucial information is unknowingly or knowingly misrepresented to you at the time of agreeing to purchase the property.

At a minimum you should have the following contingencies in your purchase and sales contract:

- **Financing** – This states that you must get a final approval for your mortgage. The preapproval mortgage most likely also had some conditions like submitting an appraisal with sufficient value and executed purchase and sales agreement.

- **Inspections** – It is typical to see a home inspection, appraisal and possibly a surveyor inspection.

- **Attorney Review** – This allows you to take the purchase and sales agreement to your attorney and get their final seal of approval as the seller might have requested some last minute changes during negotiating.

- **Review of Preliminary Title Report** – This verifies the seller has legal rights to sell the property without passing on problems such as tax liens, IRS liens etc.

- **Board Approval** – When buying a co-op there will be a board of directors who will have to approve of the transaction.

- **Appraisal** – This allows you to make sure the house will be approved for the mortgage amount you need and will verify the value you thought you were purchasing.

- **Obtaining Homeowners Insurance** – There are times when a home has certain conditions, which require more insurance coverage in addition to several different types of coverage. The price and restrictions are factors you need to know before closing the transaction.

- **Reviewing Seller's Disclosure Report** – This should have been done prior to this point, but there is no sense in taking a chance. This is also a document you would be well advised to run by your attorney.

- **Final Walk-Through** – There are horror stories galore about home buyers who did not do final a walk-through. This is a must-have AND MUST-DO contingency. .

- **Additional Contingencies** – I covered the basics, but there are many other contingencies you may wish to include depending on the seller and condition of the house. Ask your real estate agent and attorney for specific guidance regarding this situation.

How Flexible Is Too Flexible?

Jason's jaw hit the floor. He was absolutely certain that he had misheard his real estate agent. He thought there was no way possible that the seller would be willing to leave all the relatively new landscaping equipment, brand new appliances and the one hundred square foot shed to house them.

See, Jason had really piled on the contingencies because he was paying darn near to asking price. He rightfully felt that if he was paying essentially what the seller wanted, then he had to get something out of the deal. Now the truth of the matter, as his real estate agent pointed out, was that Jason was getting a heck of a deal.

I'm also pretty sure that if the seller had known Jason had spent the last two months studying how to negotiate the best deal possible, he might have bypassed his offer altogether. The fact of the matter is that Jason pushed his real estate agent to be very aggressive because he wanted to set the tone for the negotiation even though he was getting a good deal. After all he did not know the reasons for the seller taking such a loss on the sale of his home, but he knew that he should go for the gold every time he went out on the field.

Negotiating For Your Home

It is very important that you view negotiating as a vital and very important part of the home buying process. With that in mind you need to prepare yourself mentally and put on your so-called "thick-skin" because it could get ugly. However with some easy-to-follow principles you can come out on top.

We will start by taking a look at the top ten rules of negotiating real estate:

1. Gain as much knowledge as possible about the home, the seller and neighborhood.
2. Do not **EVER** offend the seller.
3. Have a back-up plan and as many alternatives as possible.
4. Listen closely and carefully.
5. Encourage your "friendly" agent to become a negotiating lion while representing you.
6. Realize no one is ever 100% on your side.
7. Always ask questions
8. Keep in mind that some deals should not be made.
9. Do not be dishonest
10. Set a timeline for your ideal time for the negotiating process.

Setting The Tone For Negotiating

Have you ever walked into a meeting and the person who is hosting the meeting lays out some ground rules for how the meeting will proceed? Well, you might want to dial it down a notch when you are meeting with your real estate agent, but you definitely want to let him or her know your preferred strategy and style. By setting the tone early on with your real estate agent you can then reinforce your suggestions for making your decisions later on.

Overview Of Negotiating Process

Every home buyer has had that butterfly in the stomach feeling when the heavens seem to open up in agreement with your idea of submitting an offer for your first home. So, we will take a look at what happens during the offer process.

1. You and your real estate agent meet to come up with a fair offer price. Your agent writes down the amount you want to pay and the terms you outline with a time limit to hear back from the seller.
2. Your agent gives the offer to the seller's agent.
3. The seller signs the offer, accepting it as it is OR rejects it in writing to your real estate agent.
4. If the seller rejects the offer he has a choice of presenting a new counteroffer with the items he wants to be changed. Normally this means a higher price than you offered.
5. Your agent presents you with the counteroffer and you accept or reject.
6. The cycle goes on and on for as long as you and the seller are willing to do so.

Negotiation Terms

When you are sitting with your real estate agent preparing your offer or sales agreement you need to understand the six major areas of negotiating in the sales contract.

- **Price or Terms**

  - **Price** – the amount that you are paying for the house. If you are paying all cash within a couple of days after signing the purchase and sales contract you should expect a lower price.
  - **Terms** – if you are asking for more repairs, different paint etc. then you are negotiating terms.

- **Your Deposit**

  You can use a larger deposit as a leverage point, which can make the sellers overlook some of your terms. However, be aware that you could lose your deposit if you do not have a real estate attorney review the contract first to make sure it's written properly.

- **Your Financing**

  If you are already prequalified for the amount of financing that you need prior to negotiating with the seller, then that puts you in better position.

  You have a weaker position if you need to have the seller give you money back at closing or have to wait for a down payment assistance grant to come through.

- **Time to close**

  The sooner you can close after your offer is accepted, the better the sellers will feel about accepting your offer.

  If you need more time, it could communicate to the sellers that you are wasting their time. Using time to your advantage is a good thing, but you need to know as much about the seller as possible before using this strategy.

- **Contingencies**

  At the minimum your sales contract must have stipulations for a clear title, home inspection, the final walk-through and the appraisal getting approved by the lender.

  Properly worded contingencies can add an extra layer of protection to you as a buyer.

- **Negotiating Strategies**

  Throughout the course of negotiating you are going to have to fight the feeling of being overwhelmed. Whenever that emotion threatens to take over just remember there are really only a couple of strategies the seller can employ. We will take a look at your negotiating options and then I will review the seller's options.

- **Buyer Offer Strategies**

  While you may feel overwhelmed by all of the options you *think* you have when negotiating, there are really only three different types of offers you as a buyer can make.

  - **Lowball** – You present an offer that is really low in comparison to what the seller is asking

  - **Almost At Asking** – Your offer is close to asking but there is little difference.

  - **Meet In The Middle** – You make an offer somewhere in between low-balling and at asking while asking for some concessions.

- **Seller Counteroffer Strategies**

  Once you submit your offer there is a tendency for buyers to over-think all of the options a seller has. In reality the seller only has a couple of choices.

  - **Highball** - The seller rejects your offer and comes back with a higher price.

  - **Meet you in the middle** – Counters back but less than asking price but a little higher than your offer price while asking for some concessions.

How You Can Win A Home Bid With A Small Deposit

Let me show you why you may be able get away with a small deposit. For the sake of this example we will assume you were selling your home and you have two parties interested in buying it for the same price. Well, obviously you will have to decide which offer to accept.

Buyer number one puts a good faith deposit of $3,000 down

on the $100,000 asking price, leaving them with only $97,000 to pay off. Buyer number two puts down $30,000 on the home, leaving them with only $70,000. Are you tempted to take buyer number two simply because they placed a larger deposit down? You might be, BUT it would probably be because you are overlooking the bigger picture. If you are the seller, you are going to get $100,000 regardless of whose offer you accept, but the determining factor is who can close!

The secret to winning a home offer bid regardless of your deposit or down payment size is to really impress upon the seller's real estate agent how quickly you can close. If you happen to find out that the seller has already closed on a second home or has to move in sixty days because of a job transfer then have your real estate agent put an earlier date into the offer contract as the closing date.

Deposit Rules: What If You Lose The Home Bid

If you should happen to lose the bid, more often than not you will get your deposit back in full. There are occasions when potential buyers will lose their earnest deposit money and your real estate agent should tell you about it ahead of time. It will also be outlined in your offer contract how much time you have to offer, counteroffer, and finalize the deal. Plus, there are contingencies wrote into the contract to protect both parties in the event the property is represented falsely.

For example, say your offer contract has 30 days to have the inspections completed and the reports returned back to you stating whether or not the property is livable, but the inspectors turn in a report within that time frame stating that the structure is not sound, it should be condemned, etc. You as the buyer could cancel the offer and get your deposit back because the decision was made within the allotted time. If you have missed all of your contingency time frames and decide the house is just is not for you and back out of the deal, you have a slim chance of getting that deposit back.

Use What You Have ...To Get What You Want!

When you are preparing with your real estate agent prior to your negotiating be sure to have all of your notes and information from your investigative work. Your research will prove valuable when you are thinking about the reasons why you are asking for a fifteen thousand dollar reduction in asking price.

7 Strategies To Make Your Offer Sizzle In A Buyers Market

Undoubtedly during your home search you will come across a home you really want to buy. Unfortunately, there may be several other buyers who feel the exact same way. If you find yourself in this situation here are some easy-to-implement tips and strategies to seize the day.

1. **Be first to act** – There is still some truth in the old saying of "the early bird gets the worm." Try to be the first buyer to seriously put in an offer and quickly get the house under contract.

2. **Ask your agent to present your offer in person** – When your agent presents your offer in person rather than fax, the sellers know you are more serious than a casual looker.

3. **Offer a higher price** – While I do have some tips to win a bid on a house without submitting an offer close to asking, there is an advantage for coming in closest to asking price because you definitely get the seller's attention.

4. **Reveal your personal reasons for buying** – When competition is fierce it is a good idea to submit your personal story and plans for the house with the offer.

5. **Minimize contingencies** – I will be the first to tell you to have as many contingencies as reasonably possible, however if you go overboard then a seller may see you as a problem buyer who is likely to cause too many problems during the transaction.

6. **Get preapproved first** – This one seems obvious yet everyday buyers submit offers without having a preapproval from a lender. Not being preapproved is the surest way to communicate to the seller's you are probably not serious about buying their home.

7. **Do not just focus on the money** – Sometimes sellers are selling their home because of issues and overall fatigue of performing ongoing maintenance. You may get an added advantage by offering to repair their problems without reducing your offer price.

Smart Home Buyer Program
<u>Step #12</u>

1. Sit down with your real estate agent and determine your offer price based on:

    - Market temperature
    - Comparable properties sold recently
    - Agent's advice
    - Seller's goal
    - Your mindset and goals

2. Determine the amount you will want put down as a good faith deposit.

3. Review the offer or purchase and sales agreement and decide which contingences your real estate agent and attorney advise as being necessary and important.

CHAPTER 12

Why a Home Inspection is Essential
Benefits of Having a Professional Inspect the Structure and Mechanical Systems Before You Settle

There are many reasons why you should get a home inspection and each one of them are valid. I will list a few that are very important. Home inspections not only verify major things such as making sure that the roof does not have leaks or rotted wood, but home inspections also verify that the home systems are working properly and verifies if the foundation your prospective home is built on is stable or crumbling.

In other words, a home inspection is simply when a licensed home inspector does a visual and functional test and observation of all the parts of the house from top to bottom including all the systems of the house. A home inspection tells you if everything in the house is working as it should be.

A traditional home inspection will give you the details about the heating and cooling systems, electrical and plumbing systems; floors, walls, the roof, ceilings, doors and windows, the home's foundation and the structural parts of the house including the basement.

99.9% Of Mortgage Lenders Do Not Require Home Inspections

Mortgage lenders do not require you to get a home inspection before they lend you money. Lenders make their decision based on the appraisal, which gives them the value of the home. However, I have seen times when the appraiser noted things on his report that needed to be fixed and upgraded and as a consequence the lender then asked for the home to be inspected. However as a rule of thumb, if you are buying a home, you will want to know as much as humanly possible about your prospective investment.

But I Have Lived Here My Whole Life!

Kyle wisely chose to be quiet as Becky verbally kicked the crap out of their appraiser about the many things he did not say was wrong with the house on the appraisal. After enduring the first two years of marriage Kyle had learned that when Becky had her mind made up it was best to let her vent her frustration.

However, the issue was that Becky's argument had two problems. The first problem was that she mistakenly assumed that the appraiser would check for holes and cracks in the foundation, termites in the walls and mold under the hardwood floors. The second problem was that she had lived in the house for the last thirty years and *she* did not even know about the cracks in the foundation right next to the washer and dryer she used weekly.

After twenty minutes of taking one of the worst verbal beatings that a person could receive the appraiser finally managed to blurt out, "For goodness sakes woman. I am an appraiser...not a home inspector! Pay the $400 and get your inspection done!"

Kyle wondered why it had taken him more than twenty minutes to defend himself with the truth about what he already knew. A home inspection would easily have caught all the problems Becky pointed out to the appraiser.

Why You Absolutely, Positively Need A Home Inspection When Buying Your First Home!

It is just good ole' fashion common sense. If you are buying a home would you want to know if everything is working as it should? What good does it do you to negotiate a great deal on the purchase price, but after moving into your new home you realize that the sellers were willing to go as low as they did because of all the problems the house has. A home inspection can also give you the leverage for negotiating for costly repairs to be corrected before agreeing on a final purchase price.

Even if you have bought ten houses and have a ton of real life experience and knowledge you still need a home inspector. The only exception is if you are a licensed home inspector and have all of the tools and training then you get a pass on this one. There are crucial pieces of knowledge and know-how that only an experienced home inspector will be able to pick up on.

A home inspector not only knows how and why things works, but he or she will know why things do not work and what has to be done to fix it.

The other important point is that as a buyer it is hard and difficult to stay level headed and detached from the emotional part of buying a home. No matter how much you try, if you find out a vital piece of information that the home seller did not disclose, it is usually perceived as being deceptive regardless if the home sellers knew about it or not.

Home Grade: Pass or Fail?

It is not possible for a home to fail a home inspection. A home inspector just tells you what is right and what is wrong and needs repairs based on the home as it is today. It is not like with the appraisal where you actually need it to come in for a certain value in order to get the mortgage. It is also not a code inspection to make sure the house is up to code according to town laws. All the home inspection does is provide detailed information about the physical condition and systems of the house.

How To Hire A Home Inspector

Just like when ordering your appraisal, your real estate agent or mortgage professional will most likely do the home inspection. However, many home buyers have more input into hiring a home inspector than with an appraiser. Even with that being said, the real estate agent and mortgage profession will usually coordinate the hiring of a home inspector for your prospective home.

If you do find yourself being the one responsible for finding, interviewing and ultimately hiring your home inspector, then you will want to make sure you follow the same three-step formula you used for finding a real estate agent, attorney and mortgage professional.

The True Cost Of A Home Inspection

The cost of a home inspection for an average single family home will be different depending on the types of tests you want performed. As a good rule of thumb, you should be prepared to spend anywhere from five to six hundred dollars to get all of the testing done.

Yes, that is a lot of money; however, do you know how much it costs to replace a septic system? Or how much it costs to upgrade an electrical system? At the end of the day you need to know any and every possible thing that can go right or wrong with the home BEFORE you buy the home. Being able to sleep at night knowing that you have made a good decision is worth many more times the cost of a home inspection. Trust me because I know from personal experience.

The other factor which makes the cost well worth the investment, is that a home inspection with a single family home in average condition only takes about three to four hours and sometimes can take up to half the day. Now let's do the math: Three to six hours to save tens of thousands of dollars and years of aggravation. Where do I sign-up? Also, if the house is smaller or is brand new then the inspection usually is done in a shorter time frame than if it is an older home with many different electrical and plumbing systems. It may also take longer if you are asking the home inspector questions about each step of the process while he's in the home. Which I recommend by the way!

The most important point to remember is that you are not paying the inspector by the hours, but you are paying him for a complete and comprehensive report about the condition of a prospective home. You are paying him for his experience, education, knowledge about homes and his overall competence. It is also of the utmost importance that you go with the home inspector and listen, ask questions and take notes.

Preparing For Your Home Inspection

You, the home inspector, the seller and maybe both real estate agents will be at the home inspection. However, regardless of who else shows up, it should definitely be you, the home inspector and seller. You should be glued to the inspector the entire time he or she is in the home, because the more eyeballs looking things over the better chance for any little detail to be reviewed. Here are some dos and don'ts when preparing to go to the inspection:

- Bring pen, paper and a list of issues your preliminary research turned up as well as the seller's disclosure so that the home inspector can address those issues while there.

- Bring a camera and video recorder, because it is important to document what you like, so you can objectively evaluate it when you are home.

- Dress comfortably, because you could be crawling in attics, underneath houses and battling through an occasional cobweb.

- By the way, DO NOT bring kids to the home inspection, because they could prevent you from paying one hundred percent attention to what is going on or they could get hurt.

Rules Of Conduct For Home Your Inspection

Now that I have told why you need a home inspection and advised you on the wisdom of attending, I will take some time to point out that it is important to be respectful of the home sellers when inspecting the home. Observe the following:

- Have special consideration for elderly sellers and tenants. Realize the sellers could have possibly raised multiple generations of their family in the home or suffered a death of a loved one.
- Honor the seller's feeling by keeping sarcastic or negative comments to yourself...at least while at the home.
- Do not go through personal stuff while there. Stick to the systems and components that the home inspector is observing.
- Wipe your feet before walking in.
- Be mindful of pets escaping outside.
- Do not touch anything that looks valuable or fragile. If you do not know about something then do not touch it!
- Find at least one thing to compliment the home seller about.

Who Gets A Copy of the Home Inspection?

This is one of the major differences from the appraisal, because the home inspector gives you the original report and you determine who receives a copy. However, you should be very careful about who gets a copy of the home inspection report, because I have seen a number of tricks that sellers have done to buyers in order to get a higher selling price.

For example:

- The seller uses the buyer's copy of the home inspection as leverage against the buyer's offering price.
- The seller intentionally understates or minimizes costly or dangerous property conditions.

Always remember that you as the buyer have the irrevocable right to receive the home inspection and determine who gets the information and when they receive it.

However, there are some findings in the home inspection, which absolutely should be disclosed to everyone ASAP. This is especially true when there is a dangerous or immediate threatening situation such as a gas leak or a faulty leaking septic tank.

How to read your home inspection report

Here is the quick cheat sheet for reading and understanding the home inspection report by breaking it apart into these categories:

- **Necessary expenses:** These are the items that you must get repaired on updated in order to make the home livable.

- **Dangerous:** Any type of exposed wiring, broker guardrails, missing steps, etc.

- **Damage Causing Parts:** These are components which are causing damage and ongoing damage to the home.

- **Non-working Parts:** All the things that are not working properly or maybe not working at all.

- **Repairs That Can Be Deferred:** These are repairs that you might want to see done, but they are not necessary for the home to be livable.

- **Anything else:** These are the miscellaneous repairs that you may want to see done at some later date to improve the overall look of your home. The house will not fall apart if these things are not done, but it would definitely make it nicer to live there.

It is important to separate the information in the home inspection report in this manner, because it is easy to get overwhelmed when seeing a home inspection for the first time. In fact if your best friend handed you a home inspection report for a brand new home and asked you for your opinion on whether or not they should buy it, you could probably say yes or no, solely based on the not-so-positive information included in EVERY home inspection report. It is important to keep this in mind when reviewing your report.

What To Watch Out For When Reading Your Inspection

In the previous section I gave you some categories to break your home inspection information into in order to make it easy-to-understand. However, there are some potential landmines hidden within home inspections such as:

- **The hidden in plain sight release permission check box** - There are some home inspection agreements that have a little check box which states that the inspector can release the home inspection report to any and all third parties without additional permission from the buyer. The reason why some home inspectors do this is to solicit business from real estate agents and other real estate professionals involved in the process. However, it can be used to give the sellers access to the report upon their request.

- **Who will be the first to see the report once it is completed?** - This goes hand in hand with the hidden check box in the example above. If the home inspector releases it to the seller's agent first then how do you think they will use it? Of course they will try to negotiate a higher selling price. That is why you must make sure that you are the first person to receive it and the one who controls who sees it.

- **What you were told at the inspection is different than what is in the report** - There are some inspectors who will tell you one thing and then write a totally different piece of information in the report. If you were told something then the report should reflect the exact same piece of information.

When To Get Additional Specialized Inspections

There may be times when your standard home inspection may not be enough. This is more common when the standard inspection turns up some facts that need further investigation. You should consider hiring additional specialists if:

- Your inspector says you should, because he noticed some major issues in one of the homes major systems.

- You have a sensitivity or allergic reaction to certain chemicals, materials, or temperature.

- You feel the home inspection report neglected to cover an issue, which you viewed as important to you.

- There are unique features to the house such as an attached dock with a boathouse, an older septic tank or in-ground swimming pool.

- The seller's disclosure mentioned some conditions that warrant further investigation.

Why You Should Get A Home Inspection When You're Bidding On A Newly Built Home

When you buy new construction or have a home custom built you have an expectation of receiving a home that is in mint-condition and that is quite a reasonable request. However, the reality is sometimes very different than the expectation. Let me give you some examples of issues you could have with a newly built home:

- **Building code violations** – usually occur in the form of loose wires, pipes that aren't long enough or improper heights on fixtures and outlets.

- **Improper ventilation issues** – the most common problem areas are the attic, roof, and kitchen when creates mold issues.

- **Roof problems** – sometimes, inferior shingles are used and are not nailed down properly.

- **Incorrect weather detailing** – creates drafts or leaks, which drive up your heating and cooling bill.

- **Uneven land, improper water main connections, or incorrectly connected sewer lines.**

Smart Home Buyer Program
<u>Step #13B</u>

1. Determine if your real estate agent or mortgage professional will order and schedule your home inspection.

2. After the home inspection is completed ask your mortgage professional for your own copy.

3. Review the home inspection and meet with your real estate agent to review your purchase and sales contract contingencies to make sure home inspection contingencies are met.

What is Coming Up Next ...

The next chapter walks you through getting your home insurance and how you can save a ton of money when insuring your dream.

CHAPTER 13

Your Legal Protection – The Title Company
The Title Attorney Oversees and Finalizes the Transaction to Protect All Parties Interest

As a first time home buyers you will have plenty of legitimate things to worry about when purchasing a new home so you will need to take as much off your plate as reasonably possible. In this chapter, I'm going to look at the huge benefit of hiring your own personal attorney when buying mistakes most first time home buyers make when they do not use a real estate lawyer, the single most important time a real estate lawyer is needed during a home purchase, and the best way to get the most out of the services your real estate lawyer is providing for the retainer you have given them.

However, I must give you a word of caution before jumping right in. There are many people (including real estate professionals) who will tell you that you do not need your own attorney to buy your first home. When someone tells you that turn, right around and ask them, "Are you willing to study for six months to take an all-day grueling test, then spend upwards of two hundred thousand dollars to attend college for six to eight years to represent me in court for two or three years in case my mortgage paperwork has a honest mistake?" If they say yes, then tell them when you are in the market to buy a house in ten years you will allow them to represent you then, but as for now you will prefer to go with an established real estate attorney. If they say no, then tell them you will feel more comfortable with someone who did!

Those people giving you that advice are also the same people who believe a closing agent or real estate attorney provided by the seller or lender actually works for you, the buyer, to protect you during the buying process. Well, let me the first to tell you that it is not true. The attorney who performs the closing for the lender or seller is there to protect the lender or seller, not you.

See everyone has an opinion about whether or not you need your own attorney when buying a home, but who will actually volunteer to be your legal representation when you are in dire straits? Now, here is the reality of risk that is associated every time anyone decides to buy a home:

- It is the biggest financial decision of your life, so you will be nervous. When most people are nervous, they forget even the simplest of things.
- You could lose your deposit because of a technicality in the wording of the contract.
- One little incorrect phrasing of a contingency could hold you legally obligated to buy a home you no longer want.
- There are some crooks in the real estate professional you will rob you blind.
- You will be legally held responsible for your home for the next thirty plus years.
- You are legally responsible if someone falls in your house, yard and possibly sidewalk in front of your house.

Whose Taxes Are These?

It came as no surprise to Andrew's after college buddies that Andrew's nickname in college had been Lucky. Even his wife Dawn had always found potentially sticky situations to magically unravel themselves when Andrew was around.

Andrew's thirty-year lucky streak was holding strong, but the day they received that infamous letter in the mail, their lives were dramatically altered. They were all set to buy their first home, but that is when Andrew's luck ran out. Apparently, the seller's attorney had forwarded a twenty five hundred dollar tax bill over to Andrew and Dawn. Although they both were surprised, they felt no real pressure to pay the bill, because after all, they did not live there last year and did not even own the house yet.

However, it was Dawn who pointed out that the letter stated the seller did not have the funds to pay the taxes prior to closing. If they did not pay the tax bill they'd never see a penny of their five thousand dollar good faith deposit they had put down. It was then that the couple decided to retain the services of a real estate

Real estate lawyers are experienced in all of the laws and regulations that are involved in the buying and selling of a home and other property. If you are like most people, then you also do not understand the complex language of the many contracts that you will be required to sign, from offering to closing, and a lawyer is the best way to make sure you are protected. They can explain all the legal terms so that you understand them. Real estate lawyers are experienced in all of the laws and regulations that are involved in the buying and selling of a home and other properties. If you are like most people, then you also do not understand the complex language of the many contracts that you will be required to sign, from offering to closing, and a lawyer is the best way to make sure you are protected. They can explain all the legal terms so that you understand them. They can also advise you on what you are looking at is the right one for you and your needs. Basically, a real estate lawyer will protect you from being tricked, robbed, or landing in financial ruin.

It never seems to fail that first-buyers run into one or two problems that will require the expertise of an attorney. It may not happen during the first property purchase or the second, but Murphy's Law tends to work in bizarre ways. Instead of tempting fate and letting a problem sneak in unannounced, reduce your chances of making a costly mistake by using a reliable and experienced real estate attorney.

Examples Of Real-Life Situations That Happen

There is nothing wrong with admitting that you need help when it comes to legal contracts. Most people do not understand what they are reading unless they already work in some form of legal profession and deal with contracts on a daily basis. It is better to retain a lawyer than take the chance of something going wrong that you cannot easily fix or that will leave you in financial ruin. Additionally, difficult sellers with unusual or unreasonable requests can be shot down when you have a lawyer with you who has the gall to say no when a real estate agent does not. When things get really strange, a lawyer in your corner will always make sure you are protected.

We will take a look at a few examples of where an attorney can definitely be a life – and financial – saver.

- You are at the closing of your home and you are presented with a different type of deed than what you and your agent originally agreed upon. If you have retained a lawyer, you would simply postpone the closing until the lawyer could look over the deed and then give you an acceptable warranty deed in place of the one that was presented to you by the seller.

- The seller of the home is procrastinating in a way that seems like they are trying to kill the sale *after* you have already signed the purchase and sale contract. The seller could be trying to accept an offer higher than the one they agreed to from you. In this case, the lawyer will step in and let the seller know that you have legal rights and that they will file a 'lis pendens'. This questions the property's ownership and could very well prove that the seller was trying to do something very underhanded.

- Your potential bargain home has a title issue that relates to the back taxes owed to the IRS by the previous owner. A capable real estate lawyer will be able to advise you on your rights and help you clear up the problem with the IRS before you close on the house. The IRS's problems are the seller's problems that they are trying to dump on you. Your lawyer could propose a compromise prior to the final closing that must be met or the deal is off until the IRS issue is fixed. If you sign off on the home before the IRS issues are resolved, you may become liable for them once you sign the papers.

- If the seller offers to do work on the home to finish something they started or to repair a problem that is outstanding, get it in writing and have the lawyer look over it to make sure everything is legal.

- Days before you close on your home your lawyer and real estate agent discover that the seller sold the house to someone else but did not file the paperwork showing the sale yet. Your lawyer could go in and file a copy of your sales contract with the court, beating out the other claimant and clouding the title for anyone else the seller may try to sell the home to.

The above situation has been prevented in many cases by the passing of a law that allows real estate lawyers to file a contract of affidavit with the courts stating that there is a sale pending on the home and that it will be closed on in a set amount of time. This helps the courts keep a track of what is going on in the real estate market and keeps double filings on one property from happening.

As you can see, having a real estate lawyer in your corner is really a good idea, especially when you're a first-time home buyer. They know and understand all of the legal wrangling that may need to take place in order to get property bought and sold without any surprises for both parties involved. As I mentioned earlier, a lawyer is not a requirement, but definitely an asset in your corner.

The Many Hats Of A Real Estate Attorney

A real estate attorney performs a variety of functions from the time they are put on retainer to the time the final paperwork is signed and you as the buyer take possession of the residence. Real estate lawyers handle contract reviews, mortgage paperwork, and researching liens and more. We will take a look at some of these functions and how they affect you in the purchasing process.

- **Real estate lawyers will review your contract and mortgage paperwork** - The wording of a real estate contract can be very hard to understand. The average person may not be able to comprehend all of the legal terminology and the services of a real estate lawyer can help you. You never want to sign any form of legal binding document without understanding what the terms and conditions really mean.

  In fact, by the time you arrive at your mortgage closing your money has most likely already been transferred from the lender who is providing your mortgage to the seller's mortgage company, hours before you ever sign the final paperwork. This is something the average investor and seller are not aware of. When you have a real estate lawyer on retainer, they will review your mortgage paperwork to make sure that there are no hidden issues that you need to be aware of before signing paperwork and taking possession of your new home. Real estate lawyers are there to protect you and your assets.

- **Real estate lawyers will look for and fix any outstanding property liens before you close** - When you prepare to purchase a home, there could be a hidden issue lurking in the background that will come to light during the selling and buying process. A real estate lawyer's job is to search the public records for any issues that may be outstanding. These ownership issues could be unpaid back taxes that are owed to the government, money that is owed for repairs, or anything that is less than legal in the eyes of the law – in other words, possible shady dealings the current homeowner has been engaged in to sell the home. While these are just a few of the issues that could surface during a title search, there could be more that could be even more devastating to you and your finances.

If your real estate lawyer finds any issues, they will alert you and the real estate agent. Searching the public records usually only takes a day or two, thanks to the connections the lawyer already has established with the local courthouses and title search companies. A title search is the most important aspect of buying a home, because of the ramifications an undiscovered issue can cause. When an issue is found and everyone is notified, the lawyer will work with you and your real estate agent to develop possible options to solve the issue. They could suggest a price reduction so the issue can be satisfied and summarily dismissed upon taking possession of the home. They will also suggest ways the seller can rectify the problem efficiently and easily without having to run around like a chicken with its head cut off. Plus, the lawyer will be able to recommend solutions that meet the requirements of your new lender. Once a legal solution is put into place, the sale can go forward without a hitch.

- **A real estate lawyer can handle all of the filing issues related to your purchase** - When you purchase a home, the deed passes to you from the seller. This deed needs to be filed with the county and state in which you live. Sometimes the property you purchase is zoned in a way that you will not be able to perform certain types of construction on it. A real estate lawyer will be able to take care of getting the property deed filed quickly and they will also be able to help you understand what the state stipulations surrounding your property are, so that you can move on with the sale armed with foreknowledge.

Here is a quick overview of the many tasks your real estate attorney/closing agent will have to do if you choose your real estate agent to perform the closing:

Selecting Your Real Estate Attorney

The guidelines for selecting a real estate attorney use the same formula for selecting each of your real estate professionals.

1. Select three local law firms to talk with.
2. One of the above should be a referral from a friend, family member or co-worker that has previously worked with the real estate attorney professional.
3. Ask for a specific person to work with then meet with them to discuss your goals and see if there is a good fit.

I realize my formula is simple, but do not minimize the effectiveness of its simplicity. As I have said before, you can't put your trust in the hands of the lender's or seller's attorney to protect you during the most exciting yet stressful financial decision of your life. You need someone in your corner in case things get rough. Someone you know has your back whenever you have a question. More importantly you need someone you can trust.

Things To Remember When Interviewing A Real Estate Attorney

The first thing you need to be aware of is that this meeting should be conducted professionally. It is a business meeting and your lawyer will be presenting him or herself with the utmost decorum. You may think that this seems a bit extreme, but it is not. Dress nicely, be on time, be cordial and polite, and above all else, be confident in yourself, your lawyer and the purchase you are about to make. Impress your lawyer and they will impress you with their knowledge and skill. Here are some specific things to do when you first meet with your lawyer.

- **Get to know your lawyer and give them the chance to get to know you.** Tell them why you are looking for a home at this particular junction in your life and why you feel you need their services. As you converse, gauge the lawyer's level of interest in taking you on as a client. This first meeting will give each of you a feel for the other before making a business agreement that should be beneficial.

- **Listen to what your attorney has to say and do not explain everything in the beginning.** Just let him know that you are a first-time home buyer and want to protect yourself while making a profit. Remember, most likely the real estate attorney has helped numerous clients that have been in the same position as you have and they understand your needs.

- **If at all possible, bring all of the documentation you have collected on the purchase with you and present it to your lawyer when asked.** By providing them with this paperwork now, you save valuable time and money running back and forth with the bits and pieces of the process.

- **Once you find a lawyer you will work with, do not be afraid to tell your lawyer everything – good and bad** – in order to make sure they are equipped with all of the information they need ahead of time. There is nothing worse than having your lawyer shocked over a piece of information that should've been revealed from the onset. Anything you say to the lawyer is confidential and will remain that way, even if you do not hire the lawyer and go with someone else.

- **Let your lawyer worry about the issues that you have no control over.** They will be able to tell you if the issues are to your benefit. This is why you have hired them. They understand the legal ramifications of many issues and they will be able to offer you possible solutions. They will help you make sure your ultimate goals are met.
- **If you feel that a lawyer is not a good fit for you, you have the right to decline their services.** The same goes for the lawyer. If the lawyer is willing to

represent you, they will be confident that everything will run smoothly. Feel free to ask them questions, including whether or not they are comfortable representing you during this transaction. Find out if the lawyer will be working on your sale exclusively or if others will be assisting and if you can meet them.

- **Ask the lawyer what their rates and fees are if you feel that the lawyer is the right one to represent you.**

- **It is okay to tell the lawyer that you want to consider their offer of representations before you sign a contract with them if you have other lawyers to speak with.** If you do decide to sign with the lawyer, have them explain their contract to you and define exactly what services they will be providing and how much they will cost. When you understand how the lawyer will work, sign the contract. Have the retainer payment on hand and request a payment schedule before leaving the office.

- **Make sure you understand when your real estate lawyer will start working on your case and when they think they will have something to report.** Let them know that you will be available to help them if required. Ask that they remain in contact even if there is nothing new going on.

Under the watchful eye of your real estate attorney, the entire transactions should move as smoothly as possible. When you are ready to close on your home, make sure you have your current photo identification with you and any closing fees in the form of certified funds. If your lawyer recommends anything else, make sure you have the documentation at the closing, just in case anything needs to be modified or added by your lawyer during the closing.

Sometimes special circumstances arise and you may need to have someone else sign your papers on your behalf. As soon as you know you will not be able to make it to the closing, contact your attorney and inform them. They will confirm with your lending institution what you will need to do to pass power of attorney to another individual – such as your spouse – or to your lawyer so that they can sign the papers on your behalf.

A real estate lawyer is a good investment all around as they can handle any and all issues that arises during the buying and selling of a home. They will ensure that all of the paperwork is legal and correct and that everything that needs to be filed is done so with the proper authorities and in a timely manner. They are well worth the investment of the retainer fee especially if something unexpected crops up. With an attorney at your side, your investment is protected.

What Exactly Does A Real Estate Attorney/Closing Agent Do?

A Real Estate Attorney does...	However, you still have to do the following...
- Reviews the title report from seller's attorney and secures you title insurance. - Tallies up the daily costs and makes adjustments to insurance, taxes and mortgage interest. - Coordinates payment for taxes and recording fees. - Completes the transfer and recording of deed. - Reviews, collects and makes sure all the necessary paperwork is there for your financing and proper disclosures. - Oversees the payment transfer to seller from your lender.	- Read every single page and document you sign. - Make sure you have a clear understanding on what you are signing off on. - Review and understand the preliminary title report and in order to understand the solutions to overcome any issues that arise. - Ask questions when you do not understand something. - Fork over the cash for the closing costs per your agreement in the purchase and sales contract. - Work together cooperatively with your appraiser, home inspector, mortgage broker and real estate agent.

CHAPTER 14

Why Not Having The Correct Six Digit Number On This Simple Little Piece of Paper Can Possibly Cause Your Entire Dream Home To Go Up In Smoke...Literally!

If you have ever been involved in a car accident in which your car was totally wrecked you most likely have a deep appreciation for full coverage insurance. The good part about having coverage from a reputable car insurance company is that you will be provided with a rental car or other transportation arrangements when accidents occur. However, in spite of their transportation arrangements you are still faced with a certain level of inconvenience and aggravation throughout the process.

Now imagine the level of frustration and aggravation you would have if your home was totally destroyed as a result of a fire or accident. Getting the correct insurance policy and fully understanding your policy is important because of two reasons. The first reason is home insurance is required by law. Second, it allows you to weather the financial storm that usually arrives on the heels of a disaster to your home.

When you buy your home you can use any home insurance provider you choose, but you do not have a choice of bypassing home insurance altogether, because your mortgage lender will require you to have adequate home insurance by the time you close.

The piece of mind you will experience will come from having adequate homeowner's insurance will:

- Protect your personal property

- Provide liability coverage
- And lastly but most importantly protect your home and home

Do not Give Me What I Paid For!

Jackie and Tony found the perfect three bedroom and two bath raised ranch after two and a half months of searching. However, the best part about their home was that the purchase price also included a detached in-law apartment, which almost seemed like its own separate little house.

When Tony called his car insurance broker to ask if they would also provide him and Jackie with home insurance he was thrilled with the monthly rate quote he received. There was only one condition, which had to be provided before he received the paperwork. The insurance agent needed a copy of the home appraisal.

Tony immediately sent over the appraisal with the check for payment and proceeded on with his day. A day or two later the insurance agent called him with some bad news. It seems that the insurance policy he had paid for would not pay out enough in the case of a disaster to rebuild both the main house and the in-law apartment. The only way the insurance broker caught it was by examining the appraisal closely.

Jackie and Tony immediately asked for additional coverage in the event of disaster. If they hadn't called and increased their coverage they would have been overcrowding their home if something would have happened in the future.

Protecting Your Home

The number one reason for having adequate homeowners insurance is providing protection for your home and additional structures like detached garage or shed. This basic coverage is the meat and potatoes of your homeowner's insurance policy. You have to remember that your house is one of the biggest financial investments you will most likely ever make, so you have to strengthen the weak spots so that you can minimize or completely eliminate any damage that might occur.

You have to make absolutely certain that you have the right type coverage and the correct amount of that coverage.

Look at these examples:

- A large tree is blown over into your living room, crashing through the roof.
- A drunk driver loses control of the steering wheel and barrels into your home.
- The hot water heater overheats and explodes.
- A lightning strike hits your house and causes a fire.

When you have the proper homeowner's policy, your policy could possibly extend coverage to you in all of the situations I just listed. You would now be covered against the random acts. The potential financial issues that are caused by random acts of nature and accidents are no longer threatening to take your home from you.

The best part about the standard homeowner's policy is that it also provides daily living expenses and short-term housing in the event the damage or cost of damage, depending on your specific homeowner's policy, means you have to live elsewhere while your home is repaired.

"Is It Time For My Annual Check-Up?"

Each and every year you should contact your insurance provider and ask them to review your policy to make sure you have the correct amount of coverage. Imagine if your $270,000 home burned down and when you filed the claim to rebuild, but you only received enough insurance money to rebuild half your home. Would that be a huge problem? Of course it would. So each year call your insurance provider and adjust your coverage accordingly.

Your Personal Property Insurance

Your normal homeowner's insurance policy also provides additional coverage to your personal possessions or property. This means the nice stuff you keep inside your home like; computer equipment, jewelry, furniture, clothing and sentimental items. There is also coverage for lawn tools and sporting equipment as well. So this means if a your kitchen and appliances are damaged by fire, your covered.

Another great part about homeowners insurance is that your coverage also extends to property not damaged on your premises meaning that your personal property can be any place in the world and still be covered. This is called your "off-premise protection". This is good news for those of us who love to travel because we can have the same peace of mind that we have at home.

Your Liability Coverage Protection

You also have what I call the "see you in court" coverage. This is the coverage for a specific level of liability that you personally cause inside or outside your home due to negligence. It is different from the unpredictable acts of danger, because you caused this particular damage.

This coverage includes paying for an attorney or legal fees as well as medical payments. In a country where it seems everyone sues for everything, this type of coverage is very important and will provide protection against the life-changing personal injury lawsuits that have become so popular. For example, say you ask your new friend over to watch the game and he stumbles over your kid's video game while walking to the bathroom and breaks his ankle. Your insurance covers his medical bills as well as numerous other costs related to his injury if you are found responsible.

What is Covered In Your Basic Insurance Policy

The regular and traditional homeowners' policy normally provides coverage for damage caused by:

- Windstorm and hail
- Lightning and Fire
- Theft, vandalism and malicious mischief.
- Explosion
- Weight of ice, snow and sleet.
- Objects falling from sky (airplane, meteorite and etc.).
- Plumbing freezing.
- Sudden and accidental damage from smoke.
- Damage from vehicles.
- Sudden and accidental tearing, cracking, burning or bulging of a steam or hot water heating system.
- Accidental discharge or overflow of water from your plumbing.
- Your personal property.
- Your negligent and unintentional act, whether on or off your property.

With your standard homeowners policy just about every calamity is covered except if it is specifically excluded in the policy. Some of the usual exclusions are:

- Floods
- War
- Earthquakes
- The land under your house
- Intentional damage
- Nuclear accident
- Structures used for business
- Sewer backup or overflow
- Cars, trucks, vans, motorcycles, aircraft and boats with anything more than a small motor.
- Wear and tear on the home including deterioration, insect and rodent infestation, settling, cracking, bulging or expansion of pavement, walls, foundations or damage from domestic animals.

- Vandalism and malicious mischief if the house has been vacant for more than 30 days.
- Theft from a house under construction
- Freezing, thawing, pressure or weight of water or ice to fence, pavement, patio, swimming pool or dock
- Animals, birds and fish
- Freezing of pipes in an unoccupied, vacant or under construction house
- Losses resulting from the failure to protect property after a loss.

It is important to remember that you can always add additional coverage to protect against most things that are on the exclusion list, but not all of them.

Saving Money When Buying Home Insurance

Here are 11 valuable secrets to help you have 100% peace of mind that your home is covered from unforeseen disasters at a price that you can afford:

Insider Secret #1 - Use A Insurance Broker

This sounds simple and basic, but you will appreciate the simplicity of it all when you save thousands of dollars per year in insurance payments. You could start by working with an insurance broker and then comparing what they offer you by asking friends and family for recommendations. Of course you can try the good ole' fashioned phone book or simply visit the National Association of Insurance Commissioners website. Checking with the state commissioner of insurance is always a good idea when you want to know the real deal on which insurance companies have the most complaints because of service or non-payment on claims.

It is also a good idea to use some of the online insurance quote companies to get a good range of what prices you can expect to pay. However, keep in mind that you have to look at more than just price alone because it does not matter how cheap the monthly payment is if they will never approve your claim to be paid out. More importantly, ask them how they determine what claims they pay out for and what you can do to make sure that your claims are handled correctly.

There is also a way to check to see if the insurance company is getting ready to go out of business or if the company is having financial problems and is not paying claims. You can check on the financial health of a company by visiting www.ambest.com or www.standardandpoors.com or simply browsing through some insurance magazines.

Insider Secret #2 - Increase Your Home Insurance Deductible

As a review, deductibles are the amount of money you must contribute towards an accident or loss before the insurance company pays the rest. As a general rule of thumb the higher your deductible, the less your monthly payment is. The reason for this reduced deductible is because you are agreeing to pay more towards any damage or loss, therefore the insurance company has to pay less. They pass on the savings to you in the form of a lower monthly payment.

These days, the majority of insurance companies do require a minimum of several hundred dollars for your deductible. You may also be able to get instant savings if you choose to increase your deductible to the next available level. However, keep in mind that if you live in an area that has many disasters you may also have separate deductibles for different kinds of loss or damage.

Another Excuse To Get The Camcorder Out

In the event of a disaster or accident insurance companies require an inventory of all your personal property and all other items as well. A pretty smart way of categorizing everything is by spending the day capturing all of your home and property on video. Be sure to check with your insurance broker to make sure they accept your video as proof of ownership.

Insider Secret #3 – The Amount You Paid Is NOT The Rebuilding Cost

The rebuilding costs are the amount that it would cost for your current home to be rebuilt if it was totally and utterly destroyed. It is important to remember that only the house itself is at risk and not the land that house sits on. That means when you calculate the value of how much insurance to buy you do not include the land value. All you will accomplish is increasing your monthly payment you have to pay.

Insider Secret #4 - Buy Your Home And Auto Policies From The Same Insurer

When at all possible bundle your auto, liability and homeowners insurance because there are some companies that will discount your premium up to 15% as a reward for giving them more of your business. However, make sure that the bundled price is actually lower than if you bought each policy separately.

Insider Secret #5 – Plan On Making Your Home More Disaster Resistant

Insurance companies give great discounts for people that put a little extra into making their home more secure and safer from natural disasters. A good example is if you install storm shutters or buy a longer lasting roof shingle. In some cases, your insurance company may give you a discount.

This is still true if you own an older home and renovate or add new materials that are stronger and better to give it additional life. There is also a huge benefit if you update all of your major electrical, plumbing and heating systems to be better prepared for future issues.

Insider Secret #6 - Improve Your Home Security

You may be able to get a sizeable discount for adding dead-bolt locks, alarm systems and smoke detectors. There are even insurance companies that offer to reduce your monthly premiums by up to 25% by installing more sophisticated fire and burglar alarms and sprinkler systems that notify the fire department or police station in the event of a break-in. However, do not get sticker-shock because those systems can cost a pretty penny and check with your insurance company before running out to purchase one.

Insider Secret #7 - Seek Out Other Discounts

You should become a discount hound. Meaning, you should regularly keep an eye out for any company that offers a discount, because not all discounts are created equal. Several companies offer discounts if your child does better in school while others offer discounts to retired people who stay home during the day because they have more time to maintain their property and discourage would-be burglars from breaking in.
You may also want to check with your employer to see if they offer a group insurance plan that is lower than your current insurance plan. You might be surprised once you do the bottom line price comparison.

Insider Secret #8 - Maintain Good Credit Scores

This one has become a huge issue for many homeowners; so do not let it bite you too. Insurance companies are now taking your credit scores into account to quote you a rate for your insurance. However, they may also use your credit scores to reduce the premium for your insurance policy, so it is a double-edged sword. If you are managing your credit scores and paying your bills on time, then you should be able to call up your insurer and request for a premium reduction because of your good credit.

In order to use this strategy you should sign up with a credit monitoring service that lets you look at your credit reports on a regular basis without lowering your scores.

Insider Secret #9 - Stay With The Same Insurer

This is the time when loyalty pays off in a big way. There are several insurance companies that give you a special discount for being loyal to them for a certain number of years.

The normal reduction you can expect is up to five percent for staying with them for five or more years and sometimes even up to ten percent if you have been with them for longer.

Insider Secret #10 - Review The Limits In Your Policy And The Value Of Your Possessions At Least Once A Year

If you are like millions of other Americans, then each year you add more and more stuff to your house. That is why it is important that once a year you take inventory and see what you have added because you will definitely want to increase your policy coverage in order to get your rightful value in case of disaster.

On the other side, you do not want to pay for a higher coverage than necessary when you got rid of things that you did not need. The best way to do this is to call your insurer or agent and tell them that you need lesser coverage because you sold some things or gave them away.

Insider Secret #10 – Consider Insurance Costs From The Very Beginning Of Buying Your Home

It is understandable that you will get excited about buying a home, but you must consider the effects that your choice will have on your insurance policy. For example, if you live near a fire department or police station you may pay less for insurance.

There may also be additional savings for you if the home you buy has newer heating, plumbing and electrical systems. You may even receive a break on the cost of your insurance if the home is built with a different type of material and construction that makes it more durable and gives it longer life. If you apply these tips you could save upwards of up to 10% on your home insurance.

Another tip that home buyers often neglect to consider is checking for an insurance claim report on the house they are considering buying. This can done easily by visiting the website for the Comprehensive Loss Underwriting Exchange (CLUE) and ordering a report to see how many claims a home has had, so you can judge the problems the home may have in the future.

It is also important to remember earthquake and flood insurance are not covered by your regular homeowner's policy. You will have to pay a little extra to get the additional insurance and you can find out all about the area you are buying in by visiting www.fema.gov/nfip.

Home Warranty Plan

I often refer to home warranties as the little known protect-me-from-the-handyman-bug protection. Here is why: Regardless of how much you plan for disasters, or inspect the appliances and hire the professionals to investigate your new home, things will happen. Sometimes you may even be the source of the problem by not knowing how to properly maintain or fix issues in your new home. But, don't be too worried about it, because there is an insurance plan that provides repairs and replacements for everything from the dishwasher to a malfunction in your electrical system.

The insurance that EVERY first-time home buyer should purchase is called a home warranty. The cost is reasonable in comparison to what is covered as a comprehensive home warranty can cost between three to five hundred dollars for a twelve or sometimes thirteen-month period.

Your home warranty coverage can financially protect you against a multitude of issues including but not limited to:

- Heating and Furnace Systems
- Air Conditioning System
- Electrical System
- Plumbing System
- Water Heater
- Whirlpool Bath Tub
- Ceiling Fans
- Burglar and Fire Alarm Systems
- Door Bells
- Dishwasher
- Oven
- Garage Door System
- Refrigerator
- Washer/Dryer
- Roof Leak Repair
- And much more

When something in your home that is covered stops working or is damaged you call your home warranty company. They will send someone out to fix or replace your equipment and you pay them a small fee ranging from seventy five to one hundred dollars for their work, even if they end up replacing and installing a brand new appliance or system. This can be a lifesaver if you bought your home and have little in the way of savings for major events.

Take some time to talk with your insurance agent to really get a good idea of the types of home warranties which are available in your area before moving forward, however whatever protection the home warranty plan provides is well worth the investment.

Smart Home Buyer Program
Step #14

1. Meet with your mortgage professional to determine if he or she has a preferred insurance provider.

2. Call your current car insurer if you have one and ask for a quote.

3. Meet with your prospective insurance agent to discuss your needs and wants for home insurance coverage.

What is Coming Up Next ...

The next chapter walks you through your home closing and what you should be aware of before attending the final signing of paperwork.

CHAPTER 15

The 10 Reasons Why You Should Hire A Speed Reader, Order Chinese Food And Wear A Bulletproof Vest To Your Closing.

Your big day is finally here. All of the gathering paperwork, shuffling through inspection reports and weekends spent looking at houses have finally come to an end. It is now time to close on your new home. There are some things which still need to be wrapped up the day of the closing and regardless of how well your real estate team plans your home closing; there will undoubtedly be some "unwrapping" that presents a surprise or two.

The Final Walk-Through

Taking one last look at the home before going to the closing is the most important task you can do next to actually signing the mortgage and ownership transfer paperwork. There are some real estate professionals who recommend doing a final walk-through five days prior to closing. My advice to you is to perform the final walk-through right before the closing is scheduled. There are too many things which could go wrong in five days, however if I walk-through the house immediately before going to the closing then I know exactly how the house will look when I get the keys in two or three hours.

You will need to have your real estate agent, the seller's agent, purchase and sales agreement and seller's disclosure when doing your final walk-through. This way you can cross-reference any of the information or observations you see with what was agreed upon. However, it is important to not over-analyze anything you see and exaggerate your observations in hope of getting a last minute deal. However, under no circumstance should you skip the final walk-through because it could cost you big-time.

"But I Do Not Like Surprises..."

Linda was bubbling with happiness and joy over navigating the entire home buying process without one mishap. Compared to what she'd seen her two best friends go through, she counted herself lucky and blessed.

She'd done it by the book. She got the mortgage first. Found a real estate agent second. Then she found a gorgeous and beautifully maintained raised ranch, which she absolutely adored. Her offer was a tad bit under asking price and was immediately accepted.

It was not until she visited her new home after the closing that she noticed something very different. She was shocked. Her bathroom was wrecked.

It seems that the sellers had ripped out the bathroom fixtures, toilet and marble countertop! She couldn't believe it! They seemed like such a nice couple every single time she met with them. Why would they do this to her?

Linda immediately called her real estate agent and attorney. Both were amazed at the audacity of the sellers. Her attorney promptly called the sellers attorney to review the purchase and sales contract and sure enough the sale of the house included all the bathroom fixtures including countertops and toilets.

Linda was relieved that she was covered but she was not prepared for the four months that it took to legally force the sellers to reimburse her for her expense of refinishing the bathroom. Every day she regretted not walking through the house one final time right before the closing.

Last Minute To-Do List

These are the series of tasks, which should be completed the last twenty-four hours prior to closing:

- **Go over the final closing amount at least three times.** – Closing costs associated with the purchase of your home are comprised of all loan fees, prepaid points, title and homeowners insurance, taxes, down payments and recording fees. You will want to double check all numbers to make sure they are roughly what you were expecting to pay. Your estimated costs which you should've received a day or two before your scheduled closing should be comparable to the fees outlined on your Good Faith Estimate, which you should have received within three days after your mortgage application, which is the law. Keep in mind that your Good Faith Estimate is just an estimate of what your costs may be. There is no real way to determine exactly what your closing costs will be prior to the day of your closing.

- **Make sure you have the appropriate payment method for closing costs.** – The payment method you are paying your closing costs with makes a big difference when it comes time to close. The seller's closing agent will not accept personal checks and will expect any needed money to either be paid by certified bank check or direct wiring of money into their account.

- **Go through the closing documents with a fine toothcomb and ask any questions you have.** – The most stressful experience in the world is having an entire roomful of people all staring at you because you have a ton of last minute questions that everyone knows should have been answered days or weeks ago. You can prevent this from happening by getting to the closing a couple of hours early to go over everything with your attorney, mortgage professional and real estate agent to make sure you have a complete and thorough understanding before you sign one document.

- **Come to closing prepared.** – Bring a recent and legible copy of a photo id as well as any receipts from any and all inspection reports you paid prior to closing.

It is also a good idea to bring any and all contracts and agreements that might have exchanged hands during the transaction such as purchase and sales agreement and seller's disclosure etc.

"Oh My Goodness...Something *Else* Popped Up"

There hasn't been one closing I have attended over the years which hasn't had at least one last-minute surprise. It comes with the territory. I have had many types of last-minute challenges for my clients in past years. Things like old collection accounts show up on credit reports, ex-spouses trying to sabotage the closing and lost paperwork. You will be happy to know that every single one of those closing was able to be completed. No matter what happens during your home buying process stay positive and optimistic. It all works out in the end.

The Closing Basics

The closing is when you sign all the mortgage and homeownership paperwork and get the keys. Behind the scenes, your lender is most likely verifying last minute information, to make sure you did not suddenly quit your job or take on more monthly debt. In order to give you a better idea of how your closing will go, we will look at the three major parts of your closing.

- **The time of your closing** - You should have set your exact or approximate closing date in your purchase and sales agreement. The date can change depending on your mortgage approval status or the seller needing additional time to clear title and such issues. However, the date on the purchase and sales agreement is the legally binding date that both parties can hold the other liable for. By the way, do not ever set the date of your closing to be on a weekend because if you have an issue with any important documents the lender will be closed until the following Monday.

- **The location of your closing** - The closing will most likely be held at the seller's attorney's office however, it can be at your attorney's office depending on what is specified in the purchase and sales agreement.

- **Who should attend the closing** – Obviously you will be there, but you should also see your real estate agent, mortgage professional and attorney. The seller, their closing agent and real estate agent should also be present. Do not be intimidated by the amount of people at your closing. Your point of view should be the more the merrier. After all if something goes wrong you want all the people who can fix the problem to be present.

At The Closing

At long last the closing day is here. No matter what time the closing is scheduled for, plan on taking the entire day off from work to avoid any running around and additional stress. I have seen closing completed in one hour and I have seen all day marathons, which take several hours and then some. The biggest difference in the length of closing time ultimately depends on you having read the documents in advance with your attorney. For whatever reason, if you have neglected to read your paperwork prior to closing, then be prepared to have a ton of questions which will dramatically slow down your closing.

Even if you have prepared for the closing as recommended, you may still have additional questions, so do not hesitate to ask them at any point during the closing. However, keep in mind that you should be prepared to get a few annoying glances and irritated looks from the seller if they felt like you did not do your homework in advance of the closing you have known about for two or three months.

Your closing is comprised of two major sections; mortgage paperwork and property ownership transfer paperwork.

You will be happy to know that you have the right to review your closing paperwork at least 24-48 hours before closing. This is the perfect time to review all of the numbers to make sure you're not being taken advantage of. You will also want to check to make sure the interest rate is fixed and that the name on the title is exactly how you want it.

Part One: The Mortgage Paperwork

The first part of your closing documents will focus on the financing side of things. The reason for this is simple; if there is no mortgage then there is no transfer of property ownership. Also keep in mind that you are buying a house for a specific amount, but when you add in the closing costs and fees your total dollar amount for buying your home is usually several thousands of dollars more than the initial purchase price. Don't get worried because it is expected and normal for this to happen.

- **Promissory Note** – This is your agreement stating you are borrowing a specific amount of money and guarantee you will pay it back as agreed upon on the form.

- **Mortgage Deed** – This is a lien placed on your property that gives the lender the right to foreclose on your house for non-payment of the mortgage.

- **Truth-In-Lending (Regulation Z) Disclosures** – This gives you all the payments you will be making on your mortgage, your interest rates and the total lifetime amount of how much you are borrowing.

- **HUD-1 Settlement Statement** – This form itemizes every penny you will be paying in connection with your mortgage. It lists every fee such as insurance premiums, attorney and lender fees, down payment amount, etc.

- **Monthly Payment Coupon** - This will be your first payment statement that will let you know what to expect to pay each month and who to mail it to.

Part Two: The Property Ownership Transfer Paperwork:

After the financing is taken care of then it is time to transfer the property ownership to you. As expected, there will be forms to sign, but there will also be paperwork such as certificates that will simply be handed over to you. Here is a list of some of the documents you should expect to see:

- **Warranty Deed** – This is the document that notifies everyone that the seller is transferring ownership of the property to you. When this document is recorded at the town or city hall it makes the transaction legally binding. It is important to note that it is when the document is recorded that it is official and NOT when it is signed.

- **Bill of Sale** – This covers all of the property and possessions that you are buying when you take over the property.

- **Affidavit of Title** – This is the seller's sworn statement that the title is in good condition and they have the legal right to sell the property to you as the owner.

- **ALTA Statement** - This is the American Land Title Association statement that gives the status of the property's title to allow you to purchase title insurance, which protects you against outside claims to your home title after the purchase.

After signing all of the documents, be sure to get your keys and exchange contact information with the seller. There will be times when you will want to call them to ask about some of the nuances of your new home that only someone who has lived there will know. Be sure to check your purchase and sales agreement to see when you have legal right to take "possession" and move into your home. Even though you have the keys, don't just assume that it is the closing date, so verify it against the date on your purchase and sales agreement. Also, be sure to know when the deed will be recorded because that will be the specific time that your purchase will be legally recognized by the town or city in which you bought your home.

Smart Home Buyer Program
Step #15

1. Go online and print out your Final Walkthrough Check List. Then inform your real estate agent and attorney that you will be performing a last-minute walk through the day of closing.

2. Meet with your mortgage professional one last time to go over the interest rate and mortgage program you will be receiving.

3. Prepare yourself and your family for the closing day shuffle. That means eat a good breakfast and get plenty of rest so that you are aware of everything that is about to take place.

What is Coming Up Next ...

The next chapter reveals how you can easily transition into your new home and neighborhood without the stresses and aggravations usually associated with moving. So continue reading...

CHAPTER 16

Settling Into And Getting
Comfortable In Your New Home

Congratulations! You just bought your first home. However, just because you have closed on your new home does not mean the work is over. In reality, your new life has just begun and there are plenty of things you will need to be concerned with. It is finally time to transition to full-fledged homeowner. Here I will examine what you will to be concerned with now that the home is yours.

Notifying Everyone That You Have Moved

By this point your immediate circle probably knows you moved, but not everyone will know your new contact information. Additionally, your creditors and banks will also need updated contact information. Here is a list of several of the places to contact:

- Utilities (electricity, water and gas)
- Bank Account Holders
- Television and internet provider
- Post Office
- Monthly subscriptions
- Department of Motor Vehicles
- Creditors (credit cards, store cards and gas cards)
- Voter's registration

It is vital that you contact every one of the companies with which you have an account, including utility companies responsible for your new home and request that service be hooked up in your name or transferred to your name on the day you take possession of the house. Try to give them as much advance time as possible so that they can get you scheduled for a service call if needed. More often than not a day or two is all you need, but it is better to err on the side of caution and give yourself more time.

Meet The Neighbors (Again)

This is the time for you to go out and reintroduce yourself and family to your new neighbors. This is one step that can make your life so much easier if done correctly. There is nothing like having someone to call when you need an extra hand around the yard or need some insider information on the neighborhood or town. Here are some ideas to get everyone together:

- Attend and volunteer for community activities
- Give your new neighbors gifts to get the wheels turning
- Host a house party for your neighbors in your new home

Announce It To The World

After your move into your new home you can simply send out emails or you can take it up a notch or two by using the following services to send out postcards or letters:

- www.movingannouncementstore.com
- www.thestationarystudio.com

You may also want to post pictures of your new home for long distance family members and friends to view by visiting:

- www.photobucket..com
- www.flikr.com
- www.imageshack.com
- Instagram
- Twitter
- Facebook

Make Sure Your Budget's In Place

As you already know, your new home comes along with new financial obligations. If you did not receive a payment coupon for your first payment at closing, you will probably get one within a day or two. Someone will inform you about your specific payment date and whom the payment will need to be addressed to. Make sure you make that payment regardless of the fact that you do not yet have a payment booklet.

Get The Kids Involved Early And Often

With all the different tasks that need to be completed it is easy to forget the little people in our lives, so here are some things to get them pumped back up:

- Throw a kid's welcome party
- Volunteer at their school
- Find out and contribute to the local playgroups

Protecting Your New Home

It is important that you are prepared for some new home jitters. Such as unknown sounds from the house settling, traffic sounds from outdoors or waking up in a new location and not knowing where you are. Do not be worried, because that is normal and to be expected. However there are some practical security and safety issues, which need to be addressed such as:

- Install new locks
- Change the alarm code
- Test the smoke detectors and indoor sprinklers
- Create an emergency escape plan in case of emergencies
- Make your home childproof
- Walk and memorize the neighborhood with the kids

- Check all the windows and doors to ensure the locks are in good shape.

Decorating Your New Home On A Budget

Most likely one of the first tests of endurance in your new home will be resisting the urge to go bananas and buy thousands of dollars worth of furniture and home accessories. While you will want to express yourself in many ways in your new home do not be too rough on your bank account. Here are some tips to decorate on a budget:

- **Take inventory** – Take a look at what you already have and then fill in the missing pieces. There are many times when we purchase things and forget about them, because we do not see them that often.

- **Research** – Shop around for the best deals. Use your family, friends and the internet to find the lowest prices and best values. This is a great time to sign-up for email notifications for special deals and prices from stores, which tend to have the best deals.

- **Prioritizing** – You need to stay focused on the essentials first and then slowly work your way through the extras as you build up your savings. This allows you to create your dream home without blowing through your money.

Be Prepared For Your Mortgage To Be Sold

You may get a letter within a month or two of moving into your new home stating that your mortgage has been sold. This is a very common practice among mortgage lenders and it is not one to be worried over. Your mortgage payment will stay the same. You will just be sending it to another a lender. Your current lender will let you know whom you are making the payment to and where to send it. Once again, you will get a payment booklet from the new lender but if it does not come by the time you need it, use the address your previous lender gave you or call your new lender for payment information.

Your payment will be tracked by the lender and they will apply your money where it needs to go appropriately. Sometimes your lender will send you a breakdown of how each penny in your payment is allotted towards the loan balance, the escrow, tax, and insurance bills. Your lender will worry about paying the real estate tax and your homeowner's insurance out of your payment every month, leaving you with two less things to worry about.

Watch Out For Rising Mortgage Payments

Occasionally you may notice an increase in your mortgage payments. This is to adjust for rising real estate and homeowners insurance cost. The amount that your mortgage goes up on a monthly basis is not usually enough to hurt you financially unless your mortgage is a variable rate loan and not a fixed rate mortgage. If you have a variable rate loan, make sure you set aside some money every month to cover any increases in the interest rate and keep your mortgage payment on time.

At the end of the year your mortgage lender will send you a year-end interest statement and account analysis. This information is needed to file your income tax and take the deductions that are due to you as a homeowner. The date you bought your house will determine whether or not you get a deduction the first year of ownership. Your tax advisor will be able to explain all of that in detail.

What is A Life Without A Big Screen TV?

James and Tonya saved fifteen thousand dollars when they bought their new home by using a down payment assistance program. James was ecstatic because they could now afford to fully furnish their new home. Tonya was a little more

See, Tonya vividly remembered all of the extra hours she'd worked over the last three years. She also remembered struggling with an older car, which was always breaking down. She suffered through it because she did not want to create another bill by buying a new car. So she wanted to limit their spending to about one thousand dollars for a living room set and five hundred dollars for a basic bed with some dressers.

James was confused and dismayed, because he felt this was their time to go all out. He wanted the big screen plasma television with the surround sound system to match. He could already envision what the oversized leather chairs would look like in his "playroom."

As the weeks rolled by James became increasingly unhappy and Tonya became more insistent upon them play it safe. However, it was not until Tonya stumbled upon an online calculator and did the math on how much they would earn in ten years if they left the money in their investment account that James fully began to realize what they would be sacrificing if they purchased all the big ticket items he felt he couldn't live without.

Prioritize Your Mortgage Each Month

Always put your mortgage at the top of the list to be paid each and every month. This will ensure that your payment is always made and it will help you maintain, build, or even repair your credit. If you ever have to take out a home equity loan, your good credit will definitely be needed. Never let anything take precedence over your mortgage payment. If you get behind, the lender has the right to start foreclosure proceedings. If your home goes into foreclosure, you will have to move out, your home will be sold to someone else, and your credit will be damaged.

If for some reason you get behind on your mortgage due to some financial problem that is beyond your control, call your lender right away. Let them know what is going on and work with them on a repayment agreement. Sometimes they will take the interest and tack on to the end of your loan, giving you a smaller payment. Sometimes they will take what you are behind and split it up over the next year, making your payment slightly higher but basically allowing you a clean slate so that you do not lose your home. Always keep the lines of communication between you and your mortgage lender open.

Save All Important Documents

When you closed on your new home there were several pieces of paperwork you will need to have in a quick and easy place to find. The major groups are:

- **Home purchase records** – This includes your loan paperwork, home insurance policy, home inspections reports, and possibly homeowner's association agreement if this applies to your home.

- **Tax Records** – As your first tax year approaches as a new homeowner you will want to make sure you have a copy of your HUD settlement form, real estate tax receipts you have paid for the year and your 1098 form.

- **Home Maintenance Records** – You will want to keep careful records of what you have been spending your money on so you will keep receipts of utility bills, service providers you have hired and the work they've done, warranty information and repair receipts.

- **Personal Records** – These are things like auto insurance policies, health insurance policies, and W2's and other income related paperwork or tax paperwork that falls in between.

Smart Home Buyer Program
<u>Chapter Summary</u>

1. Make sure you go over all of your finances with the new mortgage in place. You may want to wait until after the first month to get a gauge for your additional expenses.

2. Sit down and create a list of the items you will need and then research and prioritize what you will purchase first.

3. Collect all important documents related to your home purchase and store in a safe secure place. You will need these later.

What is Coming Up Next ...

The next chapter gives you some tips and strategies to help your Uncle Sam stay out of your bank account. So continue reading...

CHAPTER 17

The Top Ten Strategies For Keeping
Uncle Sam Out Of Your Wallet

Now that you have taken one of the most important financial steps in your life by deciding to own a home, the information I reveal to you in the next ten steps will give you the fast track to understanding how to protect yourself from the IRS, otherwise you could lose out on thousands of dollars in money.

It is a common fact that owning a home is one of the easiest ways to get the tax rewards that our government hands out. Sure, I know that we all get a great feeling of owning our own home, but the tax benefits I will reveal to you are how you calculate the true benefits of owning versus renting an apartment. After all, you most likely have been paying an arm and a leg each and every year to your good ole' Uncle Sam, but now those days are long gone! However, before you file your taxes I will reveal the grey area that you are probably not that clear on if this is your first time buying a home. Additionally if you are a first time home buyer this will definitely put you into a brand new tax filing arena because it will be your first tax return you will file after getting your new home.

By the way did you know that you are a survivor? That is right I said it. You survived and made it through the home searching and bidding ordeal. You showed determination and patience when waiting for weeks to get approved for your mortgage and all that is left now is to file your tax return as a homeowner. Just take a deep breath, sit back, relax and you will get through it just fine.

What is Tax Planning?

As a home homeowner you need to adopt a tax planning mentality. This means you should meet periodically throughout the year with your tax professional to discuss how you can minimize the amount of taxes you will be expected to pay.

Tax Tip #1 - What The Heck Is The Schedule A?

Regardless if you are a first-time homeowner or veteran homeowner who is owned many homes throughout the years, your mind probably automatically goes to "deductions" around tax time. If you are not thinking deductions around tax time then feel free to call me and I will be more than happy to take some of your deductions.

As an introduction to understanding the importance of the Schedule A, it is important to know that the big three when it comes to home deductions which are mortgage interest you paid, points you paid related to the mortgage and your real estate property taxes. However, in order to get those deductions you will need to itemize them when filing.

Most folks are a little taken back by detailing the various expenses on the 1040 Form on the Schedule A. As a new homeowner, you will feel the same butterflies in the stomach, but the difference will be that because you are prepared with knowledge then you will have butterflies because of the amount of money you will receive back.

However, I want to give you a word of caution before you begin seeing dollar signs, because you will need to spend a little time reviewing your previous filing status. The reason why I want you to take a few minutes is because you may not get the best tax breaks by itemizing your various deductions.

It is always a good idea touch in with your tax professional to learn which deduction method allows you to claim the largest deduction amount possible. It may be that the standard run-of-the-mill deduction provides a better tax break than itemizing, which means simply take the standard deduction. And do not worry, because you're not locked into any one deduction method. The IRS allows you to switch back and forth between itemizing or taking the standard deduction each and every year or take the itemization for a couple of years, and then claim the regular standard deduction amount for a period of time and then go back to itemizing again.

Regardless of which method you decide to use, the whole point of either method is to keep as much money in your pocket as possible and let the guys in Washington DC we vote in each year figure out how to budget a little better without your money!

Tax Tip #2 - The Little Known Tips For Getting The Absolute Most Out Of Your Mortgage Interest

If after meeting with your tax professional and you decide itemizing is the best option for you; then chances are that you're largest and best write-off is most likely the huge wad of interest you have paid into your mortgage. In my opinion, this is one of the most valuable tax breaks in the first several years of having a mortgage, because the majority of your monthly mortgage payments go directly towards the mountain of interest you pay.

I also feel it is important to mention your deductions are not limited to interest paid to a traditional mortgage lender. Private loans also count when it comes to deductions. Private loans are simply mortgage money loaned to you from the seller of your home.

Let me explain. A private mortgage means the seller is allowing you pay them back monthly for the amount you owe instead of using a regular mortgage bank. And just like payments to the traditional bank the interest you pay to the home seller is just as deductible as interest paid to a traditional mortgage lender. However, the mortgage loan has to use the same type of rules and guidelines as a regular mortgage bank. For example, you cannot have some weird payment schedule that you may or may not have to pay depending on variable factors.

Additionally, you get the same deduction on interest when borrowing money from people that are related to you to purchase the home. And as in a normal real estate transaction you need a knowledgeable real estate attorney to properly document the transaction and make sure that the interest rate being charged meets the minimum guidelines for mortgage lenders. You also might want to spend a few minutes meeting with your tax professional as well.

Long story short, money secured by the house is a mortgage, and thus the interest is deductible.

Tax Tip #3 – Don't Lose That HUD-1

The HUD-1 is a form that you receive at closing that itemizes each and every cost associated with your mortgage. It is very important that you do not just throw this form in the shoebox and put it in the attic. This form is what you will use to verify the correct amount of points, fees and interest that you paid and as a result will be able to deduct.

No matter what mortgage company you get your mortgage financing from, the lender is required to mail you out a form called the 1098 Form around the first month of each year. This form will let you know how much interest you have paid over the last tax year. Again, be sure to schedule some time to sit and talk with your tax professional because you must show the interest total you paid on your Schedule A.

There is a word of caution for new home buyers to not rely only on the 1098 tax information. Based on my experiences it is possible for new home buyer's to receive the form with the wrong amount.

We will look at an example:

- **Say you close on your mortgage on August 15, which means your first payment could be due on Oct. 1.**

  When you send in that first payment you will also have some interest for the month of September, but because you borrowed the money on August 15 the mortgage banks will charge you interest from August 15 to the end of August. That means that this interest is also deductible. However, some lenders will not include the interest adjustment for the first month, so you have to do the amortization charts yourself in order to catch this mistake.

The important thing to remember is the additional amount of interest will be on the HUD-1 form that you received at closing.

Tax Tip #4 - The Number One Reason Why Points Pay Off Big Time During Tax Season

Your HUD-1, and most likely the 1098 Form you will receive from your mortgage lender will show you any points that you were charged for your home loan. (Keep in mind that a mortgage point is the same as 1 percent of your mortgage amount.) And thanks to a tax break by the IRS you are allowed to deduct the points you paid for your mortgage in the same tax year you purchased the home.

There is also an important rule to remember when doing your deductions. If the home you purchased is your primary residence, meaning you live there as your home and it's not an investment, then you can chose between amortizing or deducting all your points at the same time. Most first time home buyers end up taking the option of deducting points all at the same time.

For example: by you paying 2 points on a $250,000 home loan, that $5,000 will be applied towards your total itemized deductions. You will find the total amount of points paid on your HUD-1, which might also be called loan discount fees or loan origination fees. And as a general rule of thumb: You as the buyer may still get to claim the deduction even though the seller paid the points.

Tax Tip #5 - Can You Really Deduct Your Property Taxes?

Real estate taxes are the third major home-related tax deduction. It is important to mention that this one definitely requires a tax professional to navigate, but I will review it with you so that you have some basic knowledge and have an idea.

We will start by looking at an example: Say that you have the standard tax year that begins in January and ends in December and you buy your home on July 1 and taxes are due in January. When you closed on your home you noticed on the HUD-1 that the seller had had already paid the taxes way back in January of this year for the entire year. Therefore at closing you would have to pay the seller back the money for the amount of the tax bill from July 1 to Dec. 31st. The amount you reimbursed the seller will be plainly seen on the HUD-1 and you can deduct that amount for your income tax purposes. However, there are taxes on the HUD-1 that you cannot immediately deduct.

For example, when you buy your home, you will be required to escrow your real estate taxes. This simply means that the mortgage lender receives a monthly percentage of your yearly tax amount, when you send in your regular mortgage payment each month. And in order to make sure that your escrow account is current and up to date the mortgage lender will collect about six months' worth of those payments for your escrow or reserve account. That way when it is time to pay the real estate property taxes, the mortgage lender takes the money in the escrow account and pays your tax bill.

The reason why this concept is a little advanced is because you do not get to write off the property taxes you paid because you did not actually pay it out as a closing cost. It was merely collected to be paid at a later date. It is whenever your mortgage lender pays the next tax bill for your home taxes using your escrowed money that you will get your constitutional right to deduct the amount on your tax return. Your mortgage company will usually send you the Form 1098 with the property taxes you paid. However, do not leave it up to chance. Review each and every tax bill that you receive from the county tax office to verify the amount was correct.

Tax Tip #6 - Being In The Right Place At The Right Time For Maximum Tax Deductions

As a brand new homeowner filing your taxes in a timely way is very important. As a rule of thumb, you will get the most beneficial tax deductions when you itemize, however there is another X-factor in the process. The X-factor is the actual date that you closed on your home. If you close on your home in the fall or winter of the year like November or December, then you will probably have few to no deductions for your property taxes and mortgage interest. As a result, in that case it is much smarter to use the traditional standard deduction.

The only way to know for sure is to actually meet with your tax professional before tax time when he or she has a few extra minutes to do the calculation for you. Also keep in mind when you are itemizing your deductions that there may also be non-housing items such as giving to charities paid out in the same tax year you closed on your house. This little tip is usually a mistake that first-time home buyers make when buying their home because you get so used to not keeping records because you have used good ole' fashion standard tax deduction for so long. But, those little to no deductions tax days are a thing of the past. You will quickly learn to add up every little contribution to maximize your deductible tax amount.

Where Are My Deductions?

To get the tax deduction information for homeowners directly "from the horse's mouth" you should visit www.irs.gov and download IRS Publication 530, Tax *Information For First-Time Homeowners*, and Publication 521, *Moving Expenses.*

Tax Tip #7 - The Top Deductions That First Time Home buyers Often Forget

A situation might arise where you get a line of credit or home equity loan secured by your home. If this is the case, do not just take the money and run but also consider the advantages and tax benefits that you will receive. The IRS ruled that the interest up to $100,000 on your line of credit or home equity loan is deductible. And the beauty of it is that it does not change if you use the money to buy a new car, renovate the bathrooms or put the kids the college, because the interest is all deductible. There is only one thing that matters. Is the loan secured by a home that you own?

The other deductions that first time home buyers often forget is the fact that you may get to write off a few relocation costs if you bought your house after moving to take a new job. The rule to remember is if you moved to either start a new job or relocated more than 50 miles from the old job site then you may have some additional deductions. On the other hand, if you are self-employed and working for yourself in your home then deductions that are home office based might also apply.

There are also tax breaks if you improve your home because of qualifying medical conditions.

Bonus Coverage

Due to the Taxpayer Relief Act of 1997 you do not have to pay capital gains on the first $250.000 you make on the sale of your primary residence. If you are married or filing jointly, then double that to

$500,000. In order to ride this gravy train you must have lived in your house two out of the previous five years before selling.

Tax Tip #8 - Fact or Fiction: What's Really Deductible?

There is a little word of caution when you are thinking about what you can or cannot write off in regards to your home. There will be things associated with your home purchase like your recording fees (meaning the cost of the tax office to record you as being the new owner of the house), title insurance and appraisal charges which you cannot deduct.

The list of non-deductible items also includes homeowners association fees if you live in a community that requires those fees. However, there is an exception to this one if the homeowners association pays the property tax for common areas.

Tax Tip #9 - Learn The Local Tax Exemptions

There also some good tax exemption benefits to living in certain areas that you need to be aware of. Property tax exemptions are great because they lower your overall yearly real estate tax bill. Yes, this means that you may have fewer deductions at federal tax time, but the up side is that you keep more of your money in your pocket during the year.

By the way, your property taxes are calculated based on your assessed value and the town's mill rate. The assessed value is what the town estimates your property to be valued at. The mill rate is simple a rate that is given by the town to property owners to determine their contribution to city-wide expenses. So with an exemption of $25,000 on the assessed value of your house for that was assessed at $250,000 then you only pay property taxes on $225,000 worth of value. The tax exemptions for the area you live in can be found by talking to your tax professional that you work with.

Tax Tip #10 - The Huge Benefits of Planning Your Taxes Ahead Of Time

One of the biggest tips that I can give you as a first time home buyer is to use this year's federal tax return to prepare for tax time next year. Sometime between November and December you need to meet with your tax professional and ask him or her if you may need to get more tax deductions for the current year how much of an impact that raise you received will have on your tax bill. Another good question to ask is what will be the difference if, "Can I pay my January taxes in December and what kind of impact would that have on me?"

A good little trick to use when you need an extra mortgage interest deduction in the current year is to make an extra payment before January 1st of the next year and you get to deduct it ASAP. The same also goes for paying your property taxes early. This is also the time when you will be thanking yourself that you hung onto your HUD-1 sheet, because all those extra charges you couldn't deduct before will now make a huge impact.

The biggest tax break the IRS allows us is to receive up to $250,000 in pure profit if you are single and sell your house after living in it as a primary residence two out of the last five years. If you are married and you and your spouse sell your primary home, you get to keep twice that amount tax-free. The best thing to do is to get a file cabinet or drawer especially for keeping the records of all your home-related costs. Remember to absolutely hang onto your HUD-1 as long as you own the home and even afterwards in case the IRS needs to review your tax returns at a later date.

Smart Home Buyer Program
Chapter Summary

1. Gather all of your home closing documents and store in a safe and secure place.

2. Meet with your tax professional at least twice a year to revisit your tax status and upcoming changes.

3. Be sure to maintain all receipts of any home-related expenses during the year.

IMPORTANT REAL ESTATE TERMS

Adjustable Rate Mortgage (ARM): Mortgage loans under which the interest rate is periodically adjusted to more closely coincide are agreed to at the inception of the loan.

Alternative Documentation: The use of pay stubs, W-2 forms, and bank statements in lieu of Verifications of Employment (VOE) and Verifications of Deposit (VOD) to qualify a borrower for a mortgage.

Amortization: The systematic and continuous payment of an obligation through installments until the debt has been paid in full.

Annual Percentage Rate (APR): A term used in the Truth-in-Lending Act to present the percentage relationship of the total finance charge to the amount of the loan. The APR reflects the cost of the mortgage loan as a yearly rate. It could be higher than the interest rate stated on the Note because it includes, in addition to the interest rate, loan discount points, miscellaneous fees and mortgage insurance.

Appraisal: A report made by a qualified person setting forth an opinion or estimate of property value. (Appraisal also refers to the process through which a conclusion on property value is derived.)

Appraisal Amount or Appraised Value: The fair market value of a home determined by an independent appraisal. The appraisal uses local real estate market sales activity as a major basis for valuation.

Appreciation: An increase in the value of a property due to market conditions or other causes. The opposite is depreciation.

Balloon Mortgage: A fixed-rate mortgage for a set number of years and then must be paid off in full in a single "balloon" payment. Balloon loans are popular with borrowers expecting to sell or refinance their property within a definite period of time.

Bankruptcy: Legal relief from the payment of all debts after the surrender of all assets to a court-appointed trustee. Assets are distributed to creditors as full satisfaction of debts, with certain priorities and exemptions. A person, firm or corporation may declare bankruptcy under one of several chapters of the U. S. Bankruptcy Code: Chapter 7 covers liquidation of the debtor's assets; Chapter 11 covers reorganization of bankrupt businesses; Chapter 13 covers payment of debts by individuals through a bankruptcy plan.

Cap: The limit placed on adjustments that can be made to the interest rate or payments such as the annual cap on an adjustable rate loan (ARM) or the cap on a rate over the life of the loan.

Cash-out Refinance: To refinance the mortgage on a property for more than the principal owed. This allows the borrower to get cash from the equity in their home. Loan products may vary on how much can be borrowed on a cash-out refinance.

Certified Mortgage Specialist (CMS): The Certified Mortgage Specialist is the professional sales associate who communicates the needs of the agent and borrower to the operation team.

Client Coordinator (CC): The Client Coordinator sets the tone throughout the application process and ensures that each customer is kept informed of all needs and status through clear and concise communication.

Closer: The person who coordinates the closing time with the Client Coordinator and reviews and prepares the necessary closing documents.

Closing: Also known as settlement, the finalization of the process of purchasing or refinancing real estate. The closing includes the delivery of a Deed, the signing of Notes and the disbursement of funds

Closing Costs: Costs that are due at closing, in addition to the purchase price of the property. These costs normally include, but are not limited to, origination fee, discount points, attorney's fees, costs for title insurance, surveys, recording documents, and prepayment of real estate taxes and insurance premiums held by the lender. Sometimes the seller will help the borrower pay some of these costs.

Closing Statement: An accounting of the debits and credits incurred at closing. All FHA, VA and Conventional financing loans use a Uniform Closing or Settlement Statement commonly referred to as the HUD-1.

Co-Borrower: A party who signs the mortgage note along with the primary borrower, and who also shares title to the subject real estate.

Collateral: Property pledged as security for a debt. For example, real estate that secures a mortgage. Collateral can be repossessed if the loan is not repaid.

Combined Loan To Value (CLTV): The mathematical relationship between the total of all loan amounts (first mortgage plus subordinate liens) and the value of the subject property.

Community Reinvestment Act (CRA): This act requires financial institutions to meet the credit needs of their community, including low and moderate-income sections of the local community. It also requires banks to make reports concerning their investment in the areas where they do business.

Condominium: A form of property ownership in which the

homeowner holds title to an individual dwelling unit, an undivided interest in common areas of a multi-unit project, and sometimes the exclusive use of certain limited common areas. All condominiums must meet certain investor requirements.

Conforming Loan: A loan with a mortgage amount that does not exceed that which is eligible for purchase by FNMA or FHLMC. All loans are considered either as conforming or non-conforming, also known as jumbo.

Conventional Loan: A mortgage loan not insured or guaranteed by the federal government.

Conversion Option: Options to convert an adjustable rate mortgage or balloon loan to a fixed rate mortgage under specified conditions.

Co-Signer: A party who signs the mortgage note along with the borrower, but who does not own or have any interest in the title to the property.

Creditor: A person to whom debt is owed by another person who is the "debtor".

Credit Rating: A rating given a person or company to establish credit-worthiness based upon present financial condition, experience and past credit history.

Credit Report: A document completed by a credit-reporting agency providing information about the buyer's credit cards, previous mortgage history, bank loans and public records dealing with financial matters.

Deal Structure: An Underwriters review of certain aspects of a loan application that do not meet standard guidelines.

Debt to Income Ratio: Compares the amount of monthly income to the amount the borrower will owe each month in house payment (PITI) plus other debts. The other debts may include but not limited to car payment, credit cards, alimony, child support, and personal loans. This ratio is commonly used to see if the borrower has the capacity to repay the debt.

Deed of Trust: A legal document that conveys title to real estate to a disinterested third party (trustee) who holds the title until the owner of the property has repaid the debt. In states where it is used, a Deed of Trust accomplishes essentially the same purpose as a Mortgage.

Default: Failure to comply with the terms of any agreement. In real estate, generally used in connection with a mortgage obligation to refer to the failure to comply with the terms of the Promissory Note. Most often this default is a failure to make payments, however, there are other means by which a borrower may default, such as the failure to pay real estate taxes.

Depreciation: A decline in the value of property. The opposite of appreciation.

Discount Points: A percentage of the loan amount, which is charged or credited by the lender upon making a mortgage loan. Loans that are made at the present market rate, with no points, are considered to be made at "par." Because of the lender's ability to charge or credit points on an individual loan, the lender is able to tailor a loan program and interest rate to fit the needs of each individual borrower. Discount points can be negotiated in the Purchase Contract to be paid by either the seller or the borrower.

Each point equals 1% of the mortgage loan. For example, a charge of 1 point on a $50,000 loan would result in a charge of $500; 1/2 point would be $250 ($50,000 x .50%).

Down Payment: The part of the purchase price, which the buyer pays in cash and does not finance with a mortgage.

Earnest Money: Deposit made by a purchaser of real estate as evidence of good faith.

Equal Credit Opportunity Act (ECOA): Also known as Regulation B. A federal law that prohibits a lender from discriminating in mortgage lending on the basis of race, color, religion, national origin, sex, marital status, age, income derived from public assistance programs, or previous exercise of Consumer Credit Protection Act rights.

Equity: The difference between the current market value of a property and the principal balance of all outstanding loans.

Escrow Account: An account held by the lending institution to which the borrower pays monthly installments for property taxes, insurance, and special assessments, and from which the lender disburses these sums as they become due.

Fair Credit Reporting Act: Regulated the collection and distribution of information by the consumer credit reporting industry. It also affects how financial institutions collect and convey credit information about loan applicants or borrowers.

Fair Housing Act: Prohibits the denial or variance of the terms of real estate related transactions based on race, color, religion, sex, national origin, disability, or familiar status of the credit applicant. Real estate related transactions include a mortgage, home improvement, or other loans secured by a dwelling.

Federal Home Loan Mortgage Corporation (FHLMC): Also known as Freddie Mac. A publicly owned corporation created by Congress to support the secondary mortgage market. It purchases and sells conventional residential mortgages as well as residential mortgages insured by the Federal Housing Administration (FHA) or guaranteed by the Veterans Administration (VA).

Federal National Mortgage Association (FNMA): Also known as Fannie Mae. A privately owned corporation created to support the secondary mortgage market. It adds liquidity to the mortgage market by investing in home loans through the country.

FICO Score: A credit score given to a person that establishes creditworthiness based on present financial condition, experience and past credit history.

Finance Charge: The cost of credit as a dollar amount (i.e. total amount of interest and specific other loan charges to be paid over the term of the loan and other loan charges to be paid by the borrower at closing). Loan charges include origination fees, discount points, mortgage insurance, and other applicable charges. If the seller pays any of these charges, they cannot be included in the finance charge.

Financial Statement: A summary of facts showing an individual's or company's financial condition. For individuals, it states their assets and liabilities as of a given date. For a company it should include a Profit and Loss Statement (P&L) for a certain period of time and balance sheet, stating assets and liabilities as of a given date.

First Mortgage: A real estate loan that creates a primary lien against real property.

First Rate Adjustment -- First rate adjustment after: In association with an Adjustable Rate Mortgage loan, this is the number of months after which the loan has closed when the first interest rate adjustment will occur.

First Rate Adjustment -- Maximum rate decrease: In association with an Adjustable Rate Mortgage loan, this is the most the interest rate can decrease during the first adjustment period.

First Rate Adjustment -- Maximum rate increase: In association with an Adjustable Rate Mortgage loan, this is the most the interest rate can increase during the first adjustment period.

Fixed Rate Mortgage: The type of loan where the interest rate will not change for the entire term of the loan.

Floating: The term used when a purchaser elects not to lock-in an interest rate at the time of application.

Flood Insurance: Insurance that compensates for direct physical damages by or from flood to the insured property subject to the terms, provisions, conditions and losses not covered provision of the policy. It is required for mortgages on properties located in federally designated flood areas.

Good Faith Estimate (GFE): An estimate of settlement charges paid by the borrower at closing. The Real Estate Settlement Procedures Act (RESPA) requires a Good Faith Estimate of settlement charges be provided to the borrower.

Gift Letter: A letter or affidavit that indicates that part of a borrower's down payment is supplied by relatives or friends in the form of a gift and that the gift does not have to be repaid.

Gross Income: A person's income before deduction for income taxation.

Hazard Insurance: Insurance against losses caused by perils, which are commonly covered in policies described as a "Homeowner Policy".

Home Maintenance: Costs associated with maintaining a home. This may include, but not limited to, general repairs, replacement or repair of furnace, air conditioning, roof, plumbing and electrical systems.

Home Mortgage Disclosure Act (HMDA): Also known as Regulation C. The purpose of HMDA is to provide disclosure of mortgage lending application activity (home purchase or improvement) to regulators and the public. Information is collected on each application, and is recorded on a log that is compiled to produce a report on application activity by geographic designation (census tract).

Homeowners Association (HOA): A non-profit corporation or association that manages common areas and services of a Condominium or Planned Unit Development (PUD).

Homeowners Insurance: Insurance that covers damage to the insurers' residence and liability claims made against the insured subject to the policy terms, conditions, provisions, losses not insured provision and exclusions.

Housing Expense Ratio: Ratio used to determine the borrowers capacity to repay a home loan. The ratio compares monthly income to the house payment (Principal, Interest, Taxes and Insurance).

Index: In connection with ARM loans, the external measurement used by a Lender to determine future changes which are to occur to an adjustable loan program. These will typically be published rates that are independent of the Lender's control, such as a Treasury Bill.

Initial Interest Rate: The beginning interest rate at the start of an adjustable rate mortgage (ARM). It may be lower than the fully indexed rate or "going market rate" and it will remain constant until it is adjusted up or down on the adjustment date.

Interest: The amount paid by a borrower to a lender for the use of the lender's money for a certain period of time. The amount paid by a bank on some deposit accounts.

Interest Income: The potential income from funds which would have been used for the down payment, closing costs, and any difference (increase) between monthly rental payment and monthly mortgage payment.

Interest Rate: The percentage of an amount of money that is paid for its use for a specific time; usually expressed as an annual percentage.

Judgment: Decree of a court declaring that one individual is indebted to another and fixing the amount of such indebtedness.

Jumbo Loan: A loan above the limit set by the Federal National Mortgage Association (Fannie Mae) and the Federal Home Loan Mortgage Corporation (Freddie Mac). Also referred to as a non-conforming loan.

Late Charge: An additional charge a borrower is required to pay as a penalty for failure to pay a regular mortgage loan installment when due; a penalty for a delinquent payment.

Lien: A legal claim against a property that must be paid off when the property is sold. A lien is created when you borrow money and use your home as collateral for the loan.

Life of Loan -- Maximum rate decrease: In association with an Adjustable Rate Mortgage loan, this is the most the interest can decrease over the life of the mortgage loan.

Life of Loan -- Maximum rate increase: In association with an Adjustable Rate Mortgage loan, this is the most the interest can increase over the life of the mortgage loan.

Loan Application: A source of information on which the lender bases a decision to make or not make a loan; defines the terms of the loan contract, gives the names of the borrower(s), place of employment, salary, bank accounts, credit references, real estate owned, and describes the property to be mortgaged.

Loan Balance: The amount of remaining unpaid principal balance owed by the borrower.

Loan Term: Number of years a loan is amortized. Mortgage loan terms are generally 15, 20, or 30 years.

Loan-to-Value (LTV): The ratio of the total amount borrowed on a mortgage against a property, compared to the appraised value of the property. A LTV ratio of 90 means that the borrower is borrowing 90% of the value of the property and paying 10% as a down payment. For purchases, the value of the property is the lesser of the purchase price or the appraised value. For refinances the value is determined by an appraisal.

Loan-to-Value Ratio: The ratio, expressed as a percentage, of the amount of the loan (numerator) to the value or selling price of real property (denominator). For example, if you have an $80,000 1st mortgage on a home with an appraised value of $100,000, the LTV is 80% ($80,000 / $100,000 = 80%).

Lock-In: A written agreement between the lender and borrower for a specified period of time in which the lender will hold a specific interest rate, origination and/or discount point(s).

Margin: Under the terms of an adjustable rate mortgage (ARM), the margin is a set adjustment to the index. The particular loan product determines the amount of the margin.

Median Income: The middle income level. Half of the incomes would be higher than the median income and half of the incomes would be below the median income. This is not to be confused with an average income.

Mortgage: The written instrument used to pledge a title to real estate as security for repayment of a Promissory Note.

Mortgage Insurance: Insurance written in connection with a mortgage loan that indemnifies the lender in the event of borrower default. In connection with conventional loan transactions, this insurance is commonly referred to as Private Mortgage Insurance (PMI).

Mortgage Note: A written promise to pay a sum of money at a stated interest rate during a specified term. It is typically secured by a mortgage.

Mortgage Servicing: Controlling the necessary duties of a mortgagee, such as collecting payments, releasing the lien upon payment in full, foreclosing if in default, and making sure the taxes are paid, insurance is in force, etc. The lender or a company acting for the lender, for a servicing fee, may do servicing. (Also called Loan Servicing.)

Mortgagee: The institution, group, or individual that lends money on the security of pledged real estate; the association, the lender.

Mortgagee Clause: This is the clause that is typically used for hazard insurance and flood insurance. For loans originated by the State Farm Bank it will read: State Farm Bank, F.S.B., Its Successor and/or Assigns, P.O. Box 2583, Ft. Wayne, IN 46801-2583.

Mortgagor: The owner of real estate who pledges his property as security for the repayment of a debt; the borrower.

Net Income: The difference between effective gross income and expense including taxes and insurance. The term is qualified as net income before depreciation and debt.

Non-Conforming: A loan with a mortgage amount that exceeds that which is eligible for purchase by FNMA or FHLMC. All other loans above this amount are considered to be non-conforming or jumbo loans.

Non-Owner-Occupied Property: Property purchased by a borrower not for a primary residence but as an investment with the intent of generating rental income, tax benefits, and profitable resale.

Note: A written promise by one party to pay a specific sum of money to a second party under conditions agreed upon mutually. Also called "promissory note."

Note Rate: The interest rate on the mortgage loan.

Origination Fee: A fee paid to a lender for processing a loan application; it is stated as a percentage of the mortgage amount.

Origination Process: The process in which a lender solicits business, gathers required information and commits to loan money, for the purchase of real estate.

Owner-Occupied Property: The borrower or a member of the immediate family lives in the property as a primary residence.

PITI: Term commonly used to refer to a mortgage loan payment. Acronym stands for Principal, Interest, Taxes, and Insurance.

PITI Ratio: Compares the amount of the monthly income to the amount the borrower will owe each month in principal, interest, real estate tax and insurance on a mortgage. Lenders use it in deciding whether to give the borrower a loan. Also called "income-to-debt" ratio.

Planned Unit Development (PUD): A housing project that may consist of any combination of homes (one-family to four-family), condominiums, and various other styles. In a PUD, often the individual unit and the land upon which it sits are owned by the unit/homeowner; however, the homeowner's association owns common facilities.

Pre-Approval: A process in which a customer provides appropriate information on income, debts and assets that will be used to make a credit only loan decision. The customer typically has not identified a property to be purchased, however, a specific sales price and loan amount are used to make a loan decision. (The sales price and loan amount are based on customer assumptions)

Pre-Qualification: A process designed to assist a customer in determining a maximum sales price, loan amount and PITI payment they are qualified for. A pre-qualification is not considered a loan approval. A customer would provide basic information (income, debts, assets) to be used to determine the maximum sales price, etc.

Prepaid Expenses or Prepaids: The term used to describe the funds the Lender requires to be deposited to establish the escrow account for taxes and insurance at the time of closing (also refers to Prepaid Interest).

Prepaid Interest: Interest that the borrower pays the lender before it becomes due.

Prepayment: A loan repayment made in advance of its contractual due date.

Prepayment Penalty: A penalty under a Note, Mortgage or Deed of Trust imposed when the loan is paid before its maturity date.

Principal and Interest: Two components of a monthly mortgage payment. Principal refers to the portion of the monthly payment that reduces the remaining balance for the mortgage. Interest is the fee charged for borrowing money.

Principal Balance: The outstanding balance of a mortgage, not counting interest.

Principal, Interest, Real Estate Tax, Insurance Payment: The total mortgage payment, which includes principal, interest, taxes and insurance.

Private Mortgage Insurance (PMI): Insurance against a loss by a lender in the event of default by a borrower (mortgagor). A private insurance company issues this insurance. The premium is paid by the borrower and is included in the mortgage payment.

Processing: Gathering the loan application and all required supporting documents (including the property appraisal, credit report, credit history, and income and expenses) so that a lender can consider the borrower for a loan.

Promissory Note: A document in which the borrower promises to pay a stated amount on a specific date. The note normally states the name of the lender, the terms of payment and any interest rate.

Property Taxes: Taxes assessed on real estate. Property taxes are based on valuations by local and or state governments.

Purchase Agreement: A written agreement between a buyer and seller of real property that states the price and terms of the sale.

Purchase Price: The total amount paid for a home.

Qualifying Income Ratios: Income analysis used by lenders in deciding whether to offer the borrower a loan. One type of analysis compares only the amount of the proposed monthly mortgage payment to the monthly income. Another compares the amount of the total monthly payments (for example car, credit card and proposed mortgage payments) to the monthly income.

Rate Index: An index used to adjust the interest rate of an adjustable mortgage loan.

Real Estate Appreciation Rate: Percentage increase in the value of real estate, expressed at an annual rate.

Real Estate Settlement Procedures Act (RESPA): A consumer protection law that requires, among other things, lenders to give borrowers advance notice of closing costs.

Realtor: A person licensed to negotiate and transact the sale of real estate on behalf of the property owner. A real estate broker or associate must hold active membership in a real estate board affiliated with the National Association of Realtors.

Recording Fee: The amount paid to the recorder's office in order to make a document a matter of public record.

Regulation Z: Federal Reserve regulation issued under the Truth-in-Lending Act, which, among other things, requires that a credit purchaser be advised in writing of all costs connected with the credit portion of the loan.

Rental Payment: A payment made to use another's property. The amount of the rent is determined in a contract and is typically paid monthly.

Renters Insurance: Insurance against perils, which are commonly covered in policies described as a "Renters Policy".

Repayment: The payment of a mortgage loan over a period of time established when the loan is originated.

Rescind: To avoid or cancel in such a way as to treat the contract or other object of the rescission as if it never existed.

Sales Contract: A written agreement between parties stating all terms and conditions of a sale.

Savings Rate: The interest rate a person expects to earn on a savings account or investment account.

Secondary Market: An informal market where existing mortgages are bought and sold. It is the traditional aftermarket for mortgage loans that brings together lenders that sell mortgages with lenders, investors and agencies that buy mortgages.

Seller Contribution: The seller may be paying some or all of the borrower's cost. The amount of the contribution has limitations.

Selling Costs: The costs incurred in selling a home. This could include Realtor expenses and other miscellaneous expenses such as painting or minor repairs to prepare the home for sale.

Servicing: All the management and operational procedures that the mortgage company handles for the life of the loan, up through foreclosure if necessary, including: collecting the mortgage payments, ensuring that the taxes and insurance charges are paid promptly, and sending an annual report on the mortgage and escrow accounts.

Servicing Released: A stipulation in the agreement for the sale of mortgages in which the Lender is not responsible for servicing the loan.

Servicing Retained: A loan sale in which the original lender's servicing department continues to service the loan after the sale to a secondary institution or investor.

Settlement Statement: Also referred to as a HUD-1 Settlement Statement. The complete breakdown of costs involved in the real estate transaction for both the seller and buyer.

Single-Family Attached Home: A single-family dwelling that is attached to other single-family dwellings.

Single-Family Detached Home: A freestanding dwelling for a single family

Survey: A measurement of land, prepared by a registered land surveyor, showing the location of the land with reference to known points, its dimensions and the location and dimensions of any improvements.

Subordinate Financing: An additional lien against the real estate securing borrowers' first mortgage. This lien takes second priority to the first mortgage.

Subsequent Rate Adjustment -- Maximum rate decrease: In association with an Adjustable Rate Mortgage loan, this is the most the interest rate can decrease when it is scheduled for reevaluation and possible adjustment.

Subsequent Rate Adjustment -- Maximum rate increase: In association with an Adjustable Rate Mortgage loan, this is the most the interest rate can increase when it is scheduled for reevaluation and possible adjustment.

Subsequent Rate Adjustment -- Next ARM Adjustment Date: In association with an Adjustable Rate Mortgage loan, this is the date scheduled for the next reevaluation and possible adjustment.

Subsequent Rate Adjustment -- Rate Change Frequency: In association with an Adjustable Rate Mortgage loan, this is the frequency in which possible adjustments may be made to the interest rate amount for Adjustable Rate Mortgages after the initial adjustment.

Tax Rates: Tax levied by the federal government and some states based on a person's income. Federal income tax rates vary depending on a person's adjusted gross income.

Tax Savings: The amount saved on taxes by itemizing deductions on income tax returns.

Title: The evidence to the right to or ownership in property. In the case of real estate, the documentary evidence of ownership is the title deed, which specifies in whom the legal state is vested and the history of ownership and transfers. Title may be acquired through purchase, inheritance, devise, gift, or through the foreclosure of a mortgage.

Title Insurance Policy: A contract by which the insurer, usually a title company, indicates who has legal title and agrees to pay the insured a specific amount of any loss caused by clouds, claims or defects of title to real estate, which the insured has an interest as owner, mortgagee or otherwise.

(a) Owner's Title Policy: Usually issued to the landowner himself. The owner's title insurance policy is bought and paid for only once and then continues in force without any further payment. Owner's Title Insurance policies are not assignable.

(b) Mortgagee's Title Policy: Issued to the mortgagee and terminates when the mortgage debt is paid. In the event of foreclosure, or if the mortgagee acquires title from the mortgagor in lieu of foreclosure, the policy continues in force, giving continued protection against any defects of title which existed at, or prior to, the date of the policy.

Treasury Bills: Interest bearing U.S. Government obligations sold at a weekly sale. The change in interest rates paid on these obligations is frequently used as the Rate Index for Adjustable Mortgage Loans.

Truth in Lending (TIL): The name given to the federal statues and regulations (Regulation Z) which are designed primarily to insure that prospective Borrowers of credit received credit and cost information before concluding a loan transaction.

Underwriting (Mortgage Loans): The process of evaluating a loan application to determine the risk involved for the lender. It involves an analysis of the borrower's creditworthiness and the quality of the property itself.

Verification of Deposit (VOD): Form used in mortgage lending to verify the deposits or assets of a prospective borrower when monthly statements are unavailable or unusable.

Verification of Employment (VOE): Form used in mortgage lending to verify the employment and income of a prospective borrower when pay stubs and W2 forms are unavailable or unusable.

Verification of Rent: Form used in mortgage lending to verify monthly rents paid and late payments, if any.

Special Gifts
from Kwe Parker
& Our Select Sponsors

www.ingramcontent.com/pod-product-compliance
Lightning Source LLC
Chambersburg PA
CBHW060351200326
41519CB00011BA/2112